Some years ago the church was awash in controversial books about the second coming. Each had an axe to grind for one of the theories about the nature of the millennium and about the exact order of last things. I was not sad to see those books fade away. But that left us without guides for how to use the doctrine of the second coming practically in our lives and hearts and practices. Chris Davis fills this gap wonderfully with the best practical pastoral book on the doctrine of the second coming written in years. Recommended!

—TIM KELLER, Redeemer City to City

Many of us, for many reasons, feel overwhelmed by the darkness in this cultural moment. I can think of few people better equipped or more trustworthy than Chris Davis to bring a steady ray of light by which we can more clearly see not only the future but the present. *Bright Hope for Tomorrow* isn't just about tomorrow. It's about today.

—KAREN SWALLOW PRIOR, research professor of English and Christianity and Culture, Southeastern Baptist Theological Seminary; author, *On Reading Well: Finding the Good Life through Great Books*

American Christians of the past fifty years have tended to make two mistakes when it comes to Jesus' return: either obsess over the details of when and where, or ignore its import altogether. In this biblically grounded, humble, and engaging book, pastor and writer Chris Davis helps the church recover the centrality of Christ's return and how it shapes our daily lives and affections. Jesus' return not only reorients our priorities, it also offers good news to those who labor under persecution, live with unhealed physical and emotional pain, and await justice for wrongdoing and abuse. *Bright Hope for Tomorrow* helps readers walk with a lighter step as we set our sights on the joy of seeing Jesus face to face.

—KATELYN BEATY, journalist; editor;
author, *Celebrities for Jesus*

Eschatology often signals debates and disagreements, but Chris Davis reminds us that the hope of the resurrection should make a difference in our lives today. The hope of the gospel isn't an abstraction but a powerful incentive to live for the glory of Christ and to pursue him with all our strength as long as our lives endure. Davis combines theology and practice deftly and in a way that speaks to believers as they sojourn in this earthly life.

—THOMAS R. SCHREINER, James Buchanan Harrison
Professor of New Testament Interpretation,
The Southern Baptist Theological Seminary

Fretting over possible futures, raging in the face of death, prognosticating to try to wrest some control back from the chaos of life—all these come naturally to us, whether or not we're Christian. But hope—our quiet confidence in the return of Jesus Christ and the fulfillment of God's promises through him—doesn't come naturally, which is why we need this book. In these pages, a humble and seasoned Christian pastor schools us in what Christian hope really is and how, as we fix our gaze on Christ, we may come to embody it.

—WESLEY HILL, associate professor of New
Testament, Western Theological Seminary

Bright Hope for Tomorrow is a marvelous book about a glorious topic: the return of Jesus. Chris Davis offers insights that are theologically rich, elegantly expressed, practical, and personal. In an age when far too many Christians have embraced the idols of this world, Davis reminds us we're citizens of heaven. That truth, so beautifully expressed in this book, has the power to transform lives.

—PETER WEHNER, senior fellow, The Trinity Forum; contributing opinion writer, *New York Times* and *The Atlantic*

The kingdom of the heavens is not a puzzle to solve but a real and present help to those who put their faith and trust in Jesus. Chris Davis makes this clear in *Bright Hope for Tomorrow*, a pastoral work which intends to bring heaven to readers' hearts. And it succeeds!

—MICHAEL WEAR, author, *Reclaiming Hope*

Bright Hope for Tomorrow delivers exactly what the subtitle promises. Chris Davis has created a terrific biblical guide for allowing Jesus' future return to transform us here and now. This is truly a must read!

—STEVEN TRACY, professor of theology and ethics, Phoenix Seminary

Chris has given the gift of a faithful and wonder-filled guide to better understanding, anticipating, and delighting in the hope of the gospel. *Bright Hope for Tomorrow* is both a balm for weary pilgrims and a spur to more joyfully embrace and live into the hope before us.

—CHERIE HARDER, president, The Trinity Forum

BRIGHT HOPE FOR TOMORROW

HOW ANTICIPATING JESUS' RETURN GIVES STRENGTH FOR TODAY

CHRIS DAVIS

ZONDERVAN
REFLECTIVE

ZONDERVAN REFLECTIVE

Bright Hope for Tomorrow
Copyright © 2022 by Chris Davis

Requests for information should be addressed to:
Zondervan, *3900 Sparks Dr. SE, Grand Rapids, Michigan 49546*

Zondervan titles may be purchased in bulk for educational, business, fundraising, or sales promotional use. For information, please email SpecialMarkets@Zondervan.com.

ISBN 978-0-310-13422-0 (audio)

Library of Congress Cataloging-in-Publication Data

Names: Davis, Chris, 1978- author.
Title: Bright hope for tomorrow : how anticipating Jesus' return gives strength for today / Chris Davis.
Description: Grand Rapids : Zondervan, 2022.
Identifiers: LCCN 2022014494 (print) | LCCN 2022014495 (ebook) | ISBN 9780310134190 (hardcover) | ISBN 9780310134213 (ebook)
Subjects: LCSH: Hope--Religious aspects--Christianity. | Second Advent. | BISAC: RELIGION / Christian Living / Spiritual Growth | RELIGION / Christian Theology / Christology
Classification: LCC BV4638 .D335 2022 (print) | LCC BV4638 (ebook) | DDC 234/.25--dc23/eng/20220705
LC record available at https://lccn.loc.gov/2022014494
LC ebook record available at https://lccn.loc.gov/2022014495

Published in association with the literary agency of WordServe Literary Group, Ltd., www.wordserveliterary.com.

Cover design: Micah Kandros Design
Cover art: © Traveler1116 / Getty Images; 21kompot / Shutterstock
Interior design: Sara Colley

Printed in the United States of America

22 23 24 25 26 27 28 29 30 /LSC/ 12 11 10 9 8 7 6 5 4 3 2 1

To Rachael, partner in hope

CONTENTS

PART 4: THE TRANSFORMING POWER OF HOPE

INTRODUCTION

*There are only two days on my
calendar: today and that Day.*
—attributed to Martin Luther

Have you ever needed a "that Day" to make it through today?

Ten years into my first pastorate, our church gave us a two-month sabbatical. We needed it desperately. While church life was sweet and harmonious, our family was not well. Our special-needs daughter had a mysterious throbbing ache in her mouth that caused her to cry in agony from about 8:00 p.m. to midnight every night. It baffled dentists, and none of the interventions we tried eased her pain. During that season my wife, Rachael, had a traumatic labor and delivery experience with our youngest child that required months of recovery. Meanwhile, an undiagnosed mold illness dragged me down to a depressed state such as I had never experienced before. I was constantly running on emotional fumes. This was our life in 2015: two parents physically and emotionally out of commission trying to care for four children with a host of needs.

In this fraught situation, the sabbatical took on grand

proportions for Rachael and me. It felt like a finish line, a sure refuge. To borrow from Middle Earth, it was Rivendell, where the enemy could chase us no more. For months, our daily goal was simply to make it to that day when the sabbatical would set everything right.

My guess is that you have a "that Day" that has taken on this gravitational force in your life as well. "If I know _____ is coming," you reason, "I can make it through today." You fill in the blank with the end of the semester, the promotion, the wedding day, the kids moving out of the house, retirement, or whatever day looms large over your season of life. That's when everything will change.

When the day of our sabbatical finally arrived, we launched out from Phoenix to the Smoky Mountains with high hopes. Taking in the open road and breathing in the mountain air, we knew that healing was straight ahead. Then, our first night there, my daughter started crying because her mouth hurt. My wife's recovery did not speed up. My frayed emotional state did not magically transform with a change of scenery. There was one major factor we neglected to account for in our expectations: we were taking ourselves with us on sabbatical. Two months away improved very little. "That Day" was a dud.

I write this in early 2022 when we collectively feel this dynamic regarding the coronavirus pandemic. Few of us anticipated how radically the pandemic would upend our lives. What started as a curious news report in the early months of 2020 brought life as we knew it to a grinding halt in the middle of March. By the end of the year, the sentiments of good riddance in our families and on social media were unified: "Out with 2020, bring on 2021!" In retrospect, the changing of a calendar year number should not have held such outsized promise in our minds. But that didn't stop us from feeling a breathless anticipation for what this new year would bring. Those hopes were dashed when very little changed, and by the end of 2021, the spike in the Omicron variant of COVID-19 led to a much more sober expectation for the year to come. Many dubbed the new year "2020 too."

This is the frequent outcome of our short-term hopes. The glossy brochures of an upgraded future that we imagine rarely match the reality of that day when it finally comes. "That Day" either falls flat or never arrives.

But what if our instinct isn't wrong? What if there is a day that will change everything? What if there is an event that doesn't merely loom in the far distance but is massive enough to alter how we live right now? What if, to borrow from the classic hymn "Great Is Thy Faithfulness," bright hope for tomorrow can give us strength for today?

The aim of this book is to recover what the Bible has to say about the true "that Day."

It is the day the Old Testament calls "the Day of YHWH" and the New Testament radically renames "the Day of the Lord" or "the Day of Christ."

It is the day the angels spoke of at Jesus' ascension when they said he "will come in the same way as you saw him go into heaven" (Acts 1:11).

It is the day when "the Lord himself will descend from heaven with a cry of command, with the voice of an archangel, and with the sound of the trumpet of God" (1 Thess. 4:16).

It is the day "when the Lord Jesus is revealed from heaven with his mighty angels in flaming fire" to inflict "vengeance on those who do not know God" and "to be marveled at among all who have believed" (2 Thess. 1:7–10).

It is the day when Jesus appears and "we shall see him as he is" (1 John 3:2).

This is the ultimate, the final "that Day": the day when Jesus returns.

And anticipating that day can transform how you live today.

From "Hopefully" to "Hope Fully!"

In 1 Peter 1:13, the apostle commands the church to "hope fully" on all the grace we will experience when Jesus is revealed. Those two words—hope fully—define where we are heading in this book. The goal in studying what the Bible says about Jesus' return is not to crack a secret code or connect current events with biblical prophecy but to hope fully, to live with a radical orientation around the moment we will see Jesus face to face. We hope fully when that hope transforms how we live today.

But let's be honest about how most believers think about Jesus' return. Rather than "hope fully," our posture is often better described as "hopefully." I'm not saying we deny Jesus' promise to return to make all things new. We simply keep it so far away intellectually and emotionally that it does very little to shape how we live. The word hopefully is what we use when discussing faint, distant wishes, as in, "Hopefully the lawmakers in Washington will transcend partisan grid-lock." "Hopefully my team will win the World Series." Or for those of us who are under fifty, "Hopefully Social Security will still exist when I retire." I may hope it happens, but I'm not banking on it.

That kind of "hopefully" shrug toward Jesus' coming will do nothing to change how we live in the way the New Testament authors expect a hopeful anticipation will. Their call is for us to hope *fully*. Think about what that looks like in everyday life. When our family truly believes somebody is coming over for dinner, we actually get out the vacuum cleaner and tell the kids to put down their screens because it's time to clean this place up. When you know that the big game is com-ing in four days or your wedding is coming in four months, you purchase things, you invite people, you clear your schedule, and you plan for the space to make that event happen.

Or think about how you approach a big meal. When our family lived in Arizona and our relatives were on the East Coast, we often flew through the Charlotte airport en route to seeing them. I'm a Southern boy and love good Southern cooking. So when I knew that we would be walking through the Charlotte airport past one of the best soul food restau-rants I've ever frequented, it affected what I said to the cabin crew on the airplane when they offered snacks. It didn't matter how good that cookie or bag of peanuts looked. If they weren't offering me fried chicken, collard greens, macaroni and cheese, or fried okra, I was going to say no thank you to these snacks so I could say yes to that comfort food when we landed.

That's "hope fully"—when your hope transforms how you live today. As John wrote, those who hope in Jesus' appearing purify themselves even as he is pure (1 John 3:2–3). And according to Paul, waiting for our blessed hope trains us to "renounce ungodliness and worldly passions, and to live self-controlled, upright, and godly lives in the present age" (Titus 2:12). The aim of this book is to move us from a lifeless "hopefully" to a life-changing "hope fully!"

What About the Wackos?

Before going any farther, we need to talk about the elephant in the room. Inevitably, whenever we start discussing Jesus' return, what comes to mind are all the times in church history when well-meaning but misguided teachers wrongly predicted the date of his return. Remember the book *Eighty-Eight Reasons Why the Rapture Will Be in 1988*? Or Harold Camping, whose ministry spent millions of dollars promoting May 21, 2011, as judgment day? These are not historical oddities. Such predictions and their curious mathematical formulations have come and gone throughout church history. Hippolytus (martyred around 235) predicted that the end of all things would come around five hundred years after Christ's birth,[1] while Joachim of Fiore (ca. 1135–1202) insisted that Jesus' return was imminent in his day.[2]

The most consequential predictions to our current apocalyptic milieu were delivered by William Miller. The self-educated farmer in upstate New York spent years of vigorous study on the 2,300 days of Daniel 8:14, eventually drawing the conclusion that Jesus would return in 1843. Thanks to the estimated five million tracts and books spread by Miller's publicist, "thousands (perhaps tens of thousands) waited expectantly for the Lord's return on March 21, 1843, and, when nothing happened then, on a second predicted date, October 22, 1844."[3]

The October date became known as the Great Disappointment. While some held on to revised predictions of Christ's return, giving birth to the Seventh-Day Adventist Church and influencing the rise of Jehovah's Witnesses, the predominant response was disillusionment. The Great Disappointment became an object of ridicule for skeptics and a cautionary tale for believers. Decades later, from across the pond, Charles Spurgeon warned his church not to fall into "superstitious nonsense" like the Millerites had "when they went out into the woods with ascension dresses on."[4]

As notable as these predictions are, because they required a reckoning when the day came and went, the broader story of Christian expectation has been marked by a sense that "surely it will be in our generation." Any generation looking at the wars, blights, and social upheaval of its day could assume that this means the end must be near. A 2010 survey by the Pew Research Center found that "41% of Americans believe that Jesus Christ definitely (23%) or probably (18%) will have returned to earth" by the year 2050.[5] Yet this gut feeling is as ill founded as William Miller's math.

This raises the million-dollar question: How do we hope fully in Jesus' appearing when we don't know when it will happen? It's one thing to have a date set so that the timer is ticking and we can pace our excitement like kids counting down to Christmas Day. But how do we obey Jesus' command to "Be alert!" for his return when he also tells us that "concerning that day and hour no one knows, not even the angels of heaven, nor the Son, but the Father only" (Matt. 24:36)? How do we nurture anticipation of "that Day" without any certainty that it will come in our lifetime?

Paul's Bright Hope

I believe we see how anticipating Jesus' return gives strength for today in the life of the apostle Paul. Two of Paul's earliest letters, 1 and 2 Thessalonians, are permeated with references to Jesus' coming. When I read these letters, I hear a man who is convinced that he is going to see Jesus come back in person.

In the ten years between writing 1 Thessalonians and Philippians, Paul experienced many of the persecutions and near-death experiences recorded in the later chapters of Acts: beatings, stonings, shipwrecks, imprisonments, and the incitement of more than one riot. All the while, Jesus is still in heaven and Paul is still on earth, suffering for his sake.

When you read the book of Philippians, written as Paul awaited trial in jail, you hear a shift in Paul's tone. In Philippians 1, Paul grapples with the fact that he may be executed and, consequently, see Jesus in heaven before his coming. Yet that does not stop Paul from writing, in Philippians 3, that "our citizenship is in heaven, and from it we await a Savior, the Lord Jesus Christ, who will transform our lowly body to be like his glorious body, by the power that enables him even to subject all things to himself" (Phil. 3:20–21). He awaited the Savior's return regardless of his situation.

Indeed, by the time Paul wrote his final letter, death was no longer a possibility but an imminent inevitability. In 2 Timothy 4:6–7 he declared his famous valedictory, "The time of my departure has come. I have fought the good fight, I have finished the race, I have kept the faith." In this final season of life, his sights remained set on the coming of his Savior as he anticipated receiving the crown of righteousness "which the Lord, the righteous judge, will award to me on that day, and not only to me but also to all who have loved his appearing" (2 Tim. 4:8).

To the death, Paul loved Jesus' appearing. He could approach his death with such confidence because this hope had propelled Paul to a faithful life with and for Jesus. In a touching portion of 1 Thessalonians, he imagines presenting these new believers as his "crown of boasting before our Lord Jesus at his coming" (1 Thess. 2:19). All the long hours of teaching, modeling, correcting, and encouraging would be worth it when he said, "Here they are, Jesus! I did what you told me to do!" Indeed, even when Paul knew his death would predate Jesus' return, his yearning to be with Christ—which relativized afflictions like imprisonment as light and momentary (2 Cor. 4:17)—drove his ministry to those believers. Much more than pie-in-the-sky dreaming, Paul's anticipation of seeing Jesus face to face increased his resolve to "continue with you all, for your progress and joy in the faith" (Phil. 1:25).

This kind of hope can fuel your life and ministry as well. If you find yourself feeling impatient with immature believers, if you feel the brokenness of this world in your own body, if you face afflictions because of your stand for Christ, Paul serves as a model of how a full hope in Jesus can fuel your perseverance through those difficulties. Even if Jesus comes back the day after you die, your yearning to see him face to face right now can give you the long strides needed for faithfulness to the end.

Singing Our Hope

This hope has carried believers for generations. Christ's return appears not only in the final chapters of our systematic theologies but also in the final verses of our hymns. Horatio Spafford penned "It Is Well with My Soul," one of the greatest hymns of the nineteenth century, while mourning the death of all of his children after their ship sank in the Atlantic Ocean. The hymn's final verse hopes in the coming of Jesus that will make all things well:

> And Lord, haste the day when my faith shall be sight
> The clouds be rolled back as a scroll
> The trump shall resound, and the Lord shall descend
> "Even so," it is well with my soul.[6]

Likewise, one of the greatest hymns of the twentieth century, "How Great Thou Art," locates the greatness of God not only in the works of God's hand in creation and the outpouring of God's love at the cross but in the majesty of Christ's coming. "In Christ Alone," which has drawn this generation's attention to the fullness of Christ's life and work, ends in a similar way with a hopeful look to seeing Jesus at the believer's death or the Savior's return.

"Great Is Thy Faithfulness," from which this book draws its title, does not explicitly reference the appearing of Christ but broadly points to God's past faithfulness in Christ's death ("pardon for sin and a peace that endureth"), his present faithfulness in the Spirit's indwelling ("Thine own dear presence to cheer and to guide"), and his sure faithfulness for the future ("strength for today and bright hope for tomorrow"), with an implied expectation in Jesus' return. These "blessings all mine, with ten thousand beside!"[7] became an anthem at Moody Bible Institute before the hymn gained national prominence. According to an extensive history of its place in the school's life, "The Faithfulness Song," as it was called, was a theme of hope when missionaries and Moody alumni John and Betty Stam were executed by Communist Chinese soldiers in 1934. Two decades later when five graduates from neighboring Wheaton College were murdered in the course of their missionary work in Ecuador, the song again gave voice to lament and trust in God's faithfulness. During both seasons, if the chapel leader "forgot to call for it at the end of a service, students started singing it anyway, as a spontaneous benediction before returning to class."[8]

Hymns like these have shepherded millions of believers through difficult times with the steady hope of Christ's return in power and glory. But long before these songs were being sung at Christian colleges and revival meetings, songs of hope in Jesus' coming carried along enslaved persons as they labored in fields across the American South. "In That Great Gettin' Up Morning" gave those doing oppressive work a "that Day" to anticipate with the lightning and thunder, trumpet and chariots, judgment and destruction that will accompany "the coming of the Savior." On that day they would bid an excited "fare ye well, fare ye well" to a world that had given them sorrow and loss. Like the more personal "Steal Away to Jesus," it is possible that the spiritual embedded instructions for escaping to the North in the lyrics, adding a powerful layer of short-term justice and hope to the yearning for the final, forever version Jesus will bring.

Spirituals also called individuals to let Christ's return get themselves ready. "My Lord's Comin' Again" looks to judgment and says "you had better put off lyin' shoes" and later substitutes "dancin'" and "gamblin'."[9] This longing for both personal holiness and corporate justice captures the robust effect Jesus' appearing is meant to have throughout the New Testament letters. Whether spirituals or hymns or contemporary worship songs, we can find strength for today when we sing our hope.

The Journey Ahead: Inside Out and Outside In

We have an exciting journey ahead of us. In part 1 we're going to get our bearings on where Jesus' return fits into the big picture of the biblical story. In part 2 we will focus on particular images of Jesus' return, like Jesus as a Bridegroom or Warrior King. In part 3 we're going to look at practical spiritual disciplines the New Testament lays out that help us nurture this love of Jesus' appearing. And in part 4 we will look at the ways this kind of hope should purify our hearts, propel our ministries, and fuel perseverance through affliction.

To nurture this love for Jesus' appearing, we are going to do some work from the inside out. At the end of each chapter, I will provide questions to help you identify the objects of your hope. Approach these like you would the map at a mall you're visiting for the first time. If you are looking for your favorite clothing store, you need to locate two spots on the map: the store and the "You Are Here" mark. The point of what I write in each chapter is to identify where we are going—a life of loving Jesus' appearing. For this to change you personally, the point of what you write in response to the questions is to locate where you are on the map. What are your expectations about Jesus' return? Where are you anchoring your hope right now? What do your fear and excitement say about where you would mark yourself on the map? What steps will take you from "hopefully" to "hope fully"? This will require more than a few words for answers, so find a journal or a notebook and get ready to write.

Along with the inside-out work, we'll also do some outside-in work. Chapter 8 will introduce three life rhythms God gives us in his Word to help us nurture a love for Jesus' appearing: gather, fast, and rest. These weekly disciplines can position you to focus more on the climax of God's story in

Jesus' return. These emerged from my own struggle to incorporate my new biblical discoveries into regular Christian living. God means for the return of Christ to change our lives not only in mystical or emotional ways but in our schedules and our stewarding of our desires.

My prayer is that God will stir up new and fresh affections of joy, love, and longing for Jesus in your heart as you embark on this journey. A church filled with believers eager to see their Lord will be a church of radical obedience, bold gospel proclamation, and increasing holiness. May the Spirit do this as we cry, "Come, Lord Jesus!"

PART 1

THE STORY OF HOPE

Jesus' return is not a self-contained event that we can extract from the Bible and analyze independent of the broader narrative. Rather, it is the ending of the gospel story that Christians have told for centuries: "Christ has died. Christ is risen. Christ will come again." At the same time, Jesus' return is the beginning of our new story of life forever with God in his new creation. Because of this profound role the Lord's coming plays in the biblical story, we can see this specific point of hope only in relation to the whole.

In part 1 we will look at how the promise of Jesus' appearing fits into the broader narrative of God's appearing, from the garden of Eden to the New Jerusalem. We will also explore the other revelations of Jesus in his true glory. If you have read many end-times books, this may be a different approach than you are used to. We will not be creating charts or time-lines from Old Testament prophecies, Jesus' Mount Olivet

15

Discourse, or the book of Revelation. We will not delve into questions about the millennium (the 1,000 year reign of Christ referenced in Revelation 20:1–6) or the tribulation (a time of unprecedented global suffering at the end of days). But my hope is that by tapping into the clear narrative of Scripture—the story God has been telling from beginning to end—we will find ourselves even more connected to the reality of Christ's return.

Thus we will begin by considering our own stories, our experiences of despair and hope. By doing so, I pray you will approach Jesus' return not as a puzzle to solve but as bright hope for tomorrow that gives you strength for today.

CHAPTER 1

DARK DESPAIR AND BRIGHT HOPE

God's Word teaches that the appearing of Jesus Christ in his resurrected glory is the Christian's "blessed hope" (Titus 2:13). Our hope is not vague wishful thinking or unfounded optimism. Our hope is Jesus and what he will accomplish when he returns.

Yet so often this hope in Jesus' return feels faint, distant, even irrelevant to the details of today. It twinkles like a star in the night sky that accessorizes our view but, at twenty-five light-years away, exerts no gravitational pull on us. Holding on to the hope of Jesus' return can feel like holding on to a rope when you're tubing at the lake. Sometimes you grip a sixty-foot rope that pulls you with the motorboat, each turn taking you in a new direction. Often, though, the rope feels like it is six hundred feet long. You sit on the tube, floating inert, as the sound of the boat fades into the distance. While part of the rope zips after it, hundreds of feet sit there, lifeless in the water, causing you to wonder whether the boat will actually take you anywhere.

This faint, distant feeling of hope is exposed most when we taste despair. Consider the all-too-frequent occurrences of school shootings in America. When you watch another report on the news, you immediately grieve for the families of the slain and injured students. You wonder what was going on in the life and family of the shooter. You think about the students you know—perhaps those living under your roof—and the psychological effect that active-shooter drills have on them. You live with the unwanted awareness that such a horrific event could happen in their school.

But this is not the only layer of despair you feel. If you make the questionable decision to wade into the social media response, you hear expressions of grief, thoughts and prayers for the families, and concerns about the dangers our children face. Then come the opinion pieces. Some from your tribe see this event as a clear call to change laws to make guns less accessible. Other friends believe the opposite, that the solution is putting guns in the right hands. Like a tussle over Mother's jewels at the graveside service, the communal experience of processing loss is complicated, even displaced, by ideological and political disagreement, compounding the despair that violent events will ever cease.

Other issues elicit this mingling of fear, outrage, and despair. Three of my children are African American teenagers, and the church I pastor is multiethnic, with congregants hailing from more than twenty nations. So every time I see a news report of workplace discrimination based on ethnicity,

racial disparity in home appraisals, or mistreatment of minor-
ities by law enforcement officers, despair hits close to home.
In my pastoral ministry, I have walked with dozens of abuse
survivors through their stories not only of the abuse itself but
of how those with power minimized or silenced their cries for
help. I write this during the coronavirus pandemic, when close
relationships in church and community have been ruptured by
questions of whether to wear masks or get vaccinated.

You could add further issues to the list of what causes
feelings of despair. Whatever the issue, the worst of the
despondency comes when we as followers of Jesus cannot
even agree on what the problem is and how to address it.
These matters are fracturing my evangelical tribe to such an
extent that the term evangelical has to be qualified—what
kind of evangelical are you? Pan out to our nation's intensifying
polarization on political and social matters and the disunity is
enough to drain us of all hope.

Lessons from a Funeral

When we reach our saturation point of despair over both injustice in our world and our inability to address it together, often
the Christian's last resort is "Maranatha!" borrowing from the
early church's cry, "Come, our Lord!" Perhaps you have seen
this in the comments of a social media post following a tragic
event. For some the response may feel powerful and refresh-
ing. After you've been flailing in a free fall of despondency,
the return of Christ affords a solid rock where your feet can

land. You feel relief in Christ's promise to right what is wrong and make new what is broken. You have lived long enough to know that political parties, think tanks, social-action movements, military intervention, and public outcry can put a dent in problems but never truly resolve them.

For others, "Maranatha!" feels like an excuse to avoid action now. In the film adaptation of Alice Walker's novel *The Color Purple*, Celie and Sofia respond to their respective husbands' physical abuse in opposite ways. Sofia fights back (her husband blames his shiner on the mule) while Celie endures it passively. Her reasoning? "This life be over soon. Heaven last always." Sofia is having none of it. After staving off abusive advances her whole life, she advises Celie to take matters into her own hands and "think about heaven later!" If the rope is so long that the boat is never going to pull us anywhere, we might as well start paddling the tube ourselves, right?

We are not the first ones to feel the weakness of far-off hope during a painful season of upheaval. John 11 records Jesus' delayed visit to the funeral of his friend Lazarus. The text is careful to clarify that "Lazarus had already been in the tomb four days" (John 11:17) when Jesus arrived, since rabbinical teaching of the day held that the soul attempted to reenter the body for three days.[10] For those mourning, four days dead meant as dead as dead could be. Martha and Mary tasted the depths of despair at the tomb of their deceased brother.

Jesus' exchange with Martha opens a door of understanding for how a far-off event can offer present hope. When Jesus assures Martha, "Your brother will rise again" (v. 23), she assumes that he means the final, end-times resurrection. She responds, "I know that he will rise again in the resurrection on the last day" (v. 24). Her phrase "the resurrection" was a technical term in Jewish end-times beliefs. We hear Paul use a similar phrase when he stands trial before the Sanhedrin: "It is with respect to the hope and the resurrection of the dead that I am on trial" (Acts 23:6). "The hope" and "the resurrection" were parallel terms for the Jewish belief, held by most groups except the Sadducees, that God would resurrect his people on the final day before ushering in his end-times kingdom.[11]

Martha's statement about Lazarus being raised at the resurrection was what we would call "the Sunday school answer." It was a twinkling star in her dark night of loss. It was the faint sound of the motorboat as she sat motionless on the water, watching the pile of rope next to her. It was, no doubt, a firmly held belief. But it was not a living hope.

Rather than reaffirming her Sunday school answer about a distant event, Jesus points Martha to himself: "I am the resurrection and the life." He is not interested in the theological concept of resurrection. Jesus himself, by virtue of his own resurrection, will bring about the reality of resurrection. That is why he can promise, "Whoever believes in me, though he die, yet shall he live, and everyone who lives and believes in me shall never die" (John 11:25–26).

Jesus' promise holds out hope not in the vague offer of a happier time or a better place but in the very concrete offer of himself. He is our hope. And to quote Paul, the hope Jesus offers "does not put us to shame." This isn't a capricious father's vain promise of a Hawaii vacation or the overly optimistic coach's pep talk that "we'll beat 'em next time." The grace of Jesus grants us joy through suffering now, endurance now, character now, hope now "because God's love has been poured into our hearts through the Holy Spirit who has been given to us" (Rom. 5:5). Because Jesus is our hope, our experience of Jesus' presence through the Spirit changes us now. He is the sun that keeps us in a vigorous orbit. We can feel the boat pulling us now, taking us on a ride more thrilling than anything we could generate on our own.

Hope in an Inheritance of Joy

For those tasting despair, this may sound like empty religious talk. I can appreciate your suspicion. So let's hear about this hope from one who knew tremendous suffering—Peter—and wrote to those who shared in those sufferings—the Christians in Asia Minor (modern-day Turkey). In the opening of his first letter, Peter blesses God for giving his people new birth. This new life has its origin in the past—"through the resurrection of Jesus Christ from the dead"—and its hope in the future—"to a living hope . . . to an inheritance that is imperishable, undefiled, and unfading . . . for a salvation ready to be revealed in the last time" (1 Peter 1:3–5). Their present trials, though grievous, work to purify their faith. Whatever shame, displacement, and setbacks they may experience in this life, their faith will "result in praise and glory and honor at the revelation of Jesus Christ" (v. 7).

But what exactly is Peter pointing the believers to when he speaks of these future-oriented promises—a living hope, an inheritance kept in heaven, and a salvation ready to be revealed in the last time? For the wife berated by her unbelieving husband (3:1–6), for the common laborer whose job is made a nightmare by his anti-Christian boss (2:18–20), for the Jesus followers ridiculed by old drinking buddies for not showing up at the parties anymore (4:1–6)—in what specifically are they to hope? What is the object they are to anticipate to help them through the persecution?

Peter grounds their future hope in Jesus himself, pointing to their current experience of their Lord, "whom, not seeing, you love. In whom, not now seeing but believing, you rejoice with joy inexpressible and glorified" (1:8, my trans.). We walk by faith, not by sight. We do not see Jesus, but through our faith in him we love him and taste a joy of such intensity and quality that human language cannot express it. It is a heavenly joy—a glorified joy—that we experience here on earth when we commune with our beloved Savior.

The link between this present experience and the nature of our hope, inheritance, and salvation is found in the first word of verse 9: "obtaining." When we taste joy in our communion with Jesus, Peter says we are "obtaining the outcome of your faith, the salvation of your souls." The explicit hope to which we look is inexpressible, glorious joy in our face-to-face communion with Jesus at his return. We obtain tastes of it now, like when I sneak into the kitchen to get a few bites of the roast before a big family meal. But on the day when Jesus is revealed, we will feast on the fullness of our inheritance in an imperishable, undefiled, and unfading fellowship with the Lover of our souls.

The Limits of Long-Distance Love

Until about five months before we were married, my wife, Rachael, and I were in a long-distance relationship. We were both in seminary, both working, and lived one thousand miles apart. So we found one spot in our week, Mondays at 9:00 p.m., when we could both shut off everything else and talk on the phone with each other. Rachael usually went to bed by 9:30, so she would brew a pot of very caffeinated coffee at eight to be awake for our two-hour (or longer!) conversations. These were glorious times of catching up, connecting, and deepening the joy of knowing one another. It was like our whole week revolved around those Monday nights.

But as those who have been in long-distance relationships know, those conversations were nothing like being together face to face. It was as good as it could get from a thousand miles away, but those brief days we were able to spend together in person afforded an entirely new level of joy and glory.

Fellow believer, though you have not seen Jesus, you love him. "Though you do not now see him, you believe in him and rejoice with joy that is inexpressible and filled with glory" (1 Peter 1:8). So if that is your experience of obtaining tastes of your final salvation, what will the future experience be when you see Jesus face to face? Take the greatest height of spiritual joy you have ever experienced and raise it to the power of a thousand. That is your hope. That is your inheritance—imperishable, undefiled, and unfading, kept in heaven for you. That is your salvation, ready to be revealed in the last time.

A Tale of Two Loves

What is at stake if we neglect to nurture anticipation of this face-to-face encounter? Recall that Paul, at the end of his life, identified himself among "all who have loved [Jesus'] appearing" in 2 Timothy 4:8. He knew that he would likely die before Christ returned, yet the focus of his love and anticipation remained fixed on Jesus' appearing.

In contrast, a few verses later Paul laments the fate of one whose love had shifted in the opposite direction: "Demas, in love with this present world, has deserted me and gone to Thessalonica" (2 Tim. 4:10). What Demas loved was not the "world" in terms of the physical planet but the present age. Whereas Paul's life orbited around the age that Jesus will consummate at his coming, Demas felt the gravitational pull of this life.

Paul's words about this are brief. They are suggestive, not conclusive. We do not know whether Demas abandoned the faith altogether. But what we do know is the difference in life trajectory created by these two men's divergent loves. At one time Paul and Demas shared a common purpose, a common mission, a common commitment to take the gospel of Jesus to places that had never heard the good news. Paul lists Demas as being one of "my fellow workers" (Philemon 24). He was with Paul when he wrote to the Colossians while under house arrest in Rome (Col. 4:14). These afflictions for Jesus' sake only intensified Paul's longing for Jesus' appearing. Jesus remained his center of gravity.

But somewhere along the way, Demas's center shifted. Paul writes that when Demas deserted him, he went to Thessalonica. Because of Demas's non-Jewish name and pairing with Aristarchus, who was from Thessalonica (Philemon 24; Acts 20:4), it is strongly possible that Demas was simply going home. This adds an uncomfortable normalcy to Paul's charge that Demas's decision was driven by his love for this present age. This was not Demas coming home on furlough because of a medical issue or a team conflict or one of the dozens of issues that brings missionaries home today. This was Demas deciding that he had not signed up for this level of difficulty when he joined Paul in gospel ministry. What he loved most shifted from Jesus to predictability, from the glories of Jesus' reign to the comforts of home, from the "not yet" of Jesus' return to life here and now.

We do not know the end of Demas's story. Perhaps he returned to his former life and died in obscurity. Perhaps, like John Mark, he matured after his desertion and became a devoted fellow worker again, fixed on Jesus at any cost. All we know is that Demas serves as a cautionary tale of why nurturing a love for Jesus' appearing is indispensable to finishing well in our earthly course. If Jesus' return does not hold gravitational force in your life—if the rope does not pull you—then something else will. It could be the flashy promises of money, sex, and power. Or it could be the allurement of a normal, undisrupted life.

The aim of this book is to fix your hope fully on Jesus—not merely the final event on an end-times chart but the person of Jesus. We draw near to him today in hope of the full, face-to-face encounter when he returns. As you pause to work through the following questions for reflection, may God nurture in your heart a love of Jesus' appearing, and may it begin to fuel your Christian life now.

Questions for Reflection

1. How would you describe your level of eagerness and excitement toward Jesus' return? Be honest and specific—you have to identify where you are on the map!

2. For comparison, think over the last year. What events have you anticipated the most? What emotions did you feel leading up to those events? How might you experience a similar enthusiasm for Jesus' return?

3. What issue causes you to feel despair? How do you react when someone makes the "Maranatha!" comment about that issue?

4. When you think about Christ's return and your assumptions about heaven attached to it, what are the images and impressions that immediately come to mind?

5. According to the following passage, what is the defining experience of our salvation? "Though you have not seen [Jesus Christ], you love him. Though you do not now see him, you believe in him and rejoice with joy that is inexpressible and filled with glory, obtaining the outcome of your faith, the salvation of your souls" (1 Peter 1:8–9).

6. How could this truth change how you view heaven, and create excitement for Jesus' return?

CHAPTER 2

THE DAY OF
THE LORD

A bank teller in Dayton, Ohio, dials 911 for medical inter-vention when a man in the lobby, Robert Strank, nearly passes out and asks the teller to call for help.

Police in Des Moines, Iowa, respond to a panicked request from William Kline after his ten-year-old son, Brian, hand-cuffs the two together, not realizing that William kept the cuffs from his old security job but not the keys.

In Pretoria, South Africa, passersby and police come to the aid of a man who has been stuck in a car for an hour and a half, banging on the windows and pleading for help.

In each of these accounts, you would assume that the presence of those arriving to help would be a good thing, wouldn't you? Yet in each case there is more to the story.

The arrival of paramedics to the Huntington Bank would have been great news if Robert Strank, for inexplicable rea-sons, had not made a second request of the teller, this time handing a note demanding cash. Whether or not the fainting spell was part of the attempted bank robbery, Strank didn't realize that a 911 call would result in both paramedics and police arriving. Once his medical status was given the all clear, the officers took Strank into custody.[12]

The officers who successfully uncuffed Brian from his dad had a good laugh with the pair about this innocent mishap on Father's Day, of all days. After they left, they ran William's name through their the police database, per department protocol. The search revealed that the father had two outstanding warrants for his arrest. So they went back inside to cuff him for real this time.[13]

And what of the poor man stuck in the car in South Africa? As it turns out, he was a thief posing as a car guard who used a jamming device to enter the car to grab any valuables he might find there. But the autolock function of the BMW 3 Series sedan kicked in and left the man with no way to get out. When Nosipho Mckay returned to her car, she granted the man's request for help, at which point the police promptly arrested him.[14]

Good News or Bad News?

With these stories in mind, let me ask a question you may not have considered before: Is Jesus' return a good thing?

If you are hesitating, wondering whether the answer is more complicated than yes or no, you are on to something. Jesus' return is a development in a broader narrative thread. Since the garden of Eden, the appearing of God's presence can be beautiful or terrible. When we trace that thread, we quickly realize that Jesus' showing up in person is not simply the cue for "and they all lived happily ever after."

When Jesus returns, he will return as the Lover of our souls, the Bridegroom returning for his bride, the Resurrecting One who makes all things new. He will also return as the conquering King and the righteous Judge. (We will view each of these portraits more fully in part 2.) His appearing could be the best news or the worst news of a person's life. This gap between the beautiful and the terrible has profound implications for how we live.

To get the broad scope of this story, we'll start at the beginning of the biblical narrative, trace the progression of God's appearing to "the day of the Lord," then see how Jesus' first and second comings fit into this picture. Along the way we will learn how his return can become our greatest hope rather than our greatest dread.

The Holy, Burning Presence

Let's begin with Adam and Eve in the garden of Eden. Was God's presence in the garden rewarding or punishing? The answer depends on whether they have eaten the forbidden fruit. Presumably, before their disobedience, Adam and Eve would have "heard the sound of the LORD God walking in the garden in the cool of the day" and joined him, walking with God in sweet communion. But after they had spurned his authority and broken his one commandment, "the man and his wife hid themselves from the presence of the LORD God among the trees of the garden" (Gen. 3:8). Because of their sin, being in God's presence was an experience of fear, guilt, and shame.

This theme continues through the biblical story. Whether in the great flood or at Sodom and Gomorrah, God's presence meant rescue for some and judgment for others. This was most pronounced in the Exodus, when Yahweh's appearance meant deliverance for the Hebrew slaves but death for Pharaoh's army. The children of Israel observed God's plagues on Egypt, culminating in the death of all firstborn sons in households whose doorposts and lintel were not covered with the lamb's blood. They watched the cloud and fire separate them from the charging Egyptian army while Moses held up his staff and Yahweh parted the Red Sea. After walking through on dry ground, they saw the most powerful military force in the world reduced to flotsam and jetsam.

But what caused the children of Abraham to tremble even more than God's deeds was their encounter with God himself. Yahweh informed Moses that "on the third day the LORD will come down on Mount Sinai in the sight of all the people" (Ex. 19:11) The verses that follow recount a multisensory experience of "thunders and lightnings," "a thick cloud," and "a very loud trumpet blast" (v. 16). Yahweh descended onto the mountain "in fire," so that the mountain smoked and shook (v. 18). Appropriately, "all the people in the camp trembled" (v. 16).

Before we move on in the story, let us pause to consider the awe and sobriety that should be layered over our eagerness to be in God's presence. Despite modern impulses to downplay the less socially acceptable attributes of the Almighty, we must either take God as he reveals himself or not take him at all. He is loving, faithful, compassionate, and self-giving. He redeemed the oppressed Hebrew slaves. He provided for their every need supernaturally. And this God is holy, vengeful, and unrelenting in his commitment to his own glory. Yahweh "your God is a consuming fire, a jealous God" (Deut. 4:24). Being in the presence of such a God should fill us with as much reverence as it does delight.

The Day of the LORD

Following the trembling encounter with Yahweh in Exodus 19 is the giving of the law in Exodus 20. Beginning with the Ten Commandments, God made clear to his people how they were to live faithfully in their covenant relationship with their Redeemer. Yet almost as soon as the law was given (remember Eden and the forbidden fruit?), God's people were breaking it. Moses couldn't even get down from the mountain before the children of Israel were dancing around the golden calf.

So Moses became not only lawgiver but also prophet, one who called God's people to faithful obedience to their covenant God. Over the centuries that followed, Joshua, Samuel, Elijah, and other prophets served in a similar way as covenant enforcers. Eventually the prophets began writing down their proclamations against God's people, and their warnings took on a forward-looking character as they pointed God's people to "the day of the LORD."

The day the prophets warned of was the day when Yahweh would come in all of his holy, burning glory. It is "the day of I AM's glory when he punishes the wicked and rewards the faithful, making all things new in the final cosmos as the home of righteousness."[15] As in Eden, Sodom, or Egypt, this coming of God's presence would mean disaster for the faithless and deliverance for the faithful. Read slowly over these prophetic pronouncements and feel their urgency and weight:

- "Wail, for the day of the LORD is near; as destruction from the Almighty it will come!" (Isa. 13:6).
- "Behold, the day of the LORD comes, cruel, with wrath and fierce anger, to make the land a desolation and to destroy its sinners from it" (Isa. 13:9).
- "That day is the day of the Lord GOD of hosts, a day of vengeance, to avenge himself on his foes. The sword shall devour and be sated and drink its fill of their blood" (Jer. 46:10).
- "The LORD utters his voice before his army, for his camp is exceedingly great; he who executes his word is powerful. For the day of the LORD is great and very awesome; who can endure it?" (Joel 2:11).
- "Woe to you who desire the day of the LORD! Why would you have the day of the LORD? It is darkness, and not light, as if a man fled from a lion, and a bear met him, or went into the house and leaned his hand against the wall, and a serpent bit him. Is not the day of the LORD darkness, and not light, and gloom with no brightness in it?" (Amos 5:18–20).

The tone is unmistakable. The prophets spoke to God's disobedient people, reminding them that an encounter with God while rejecting his authority is a supernatural disaster waiting to happen. Many of the pronouncements accompanied military or agricultural crises (such as the locust plague in Joel), identifying the devastation as only a foretaste of the wrath of the final day.

For our study, the most important reference to the day of the LORD is the final one, the next-to-the-last verse of the Old Testament: "Behold, I will send you Elijah the prophet before the great and awesome day of the LORD comes" (Mal. 4:5). The last of the writing prophets clearly indicated that the day of the LORD had not yet come but would be signaled by the coming of Elijah the prophet.

Fulfillment and Plot Twist

And indeed, Elijah the prophet came. John the Baptist arrived on the scene, preaching a baptism of repentance and the coming of the kingdom of God. Jesus plainly taught that "John the Baptist . . . is Elijah who is to come" (Matt. 11:12–14; see also 17:9–13 and Mark 9:9–13).

This clear teaching, plus the host of prophetic references to the epic nature of the day of the LORD, should create sympathy for the disciples who always seemed to be champing at the bit for Jesus to defeat the Romans. By the time Jesus' ministry began, the Romans had ruled over the Jewish people for nearly a century, making them captives in their own land and subjecting them to harsh taxation and cruel treatment. If John the Baptist was Elijah, and Jesus was the Lord, what was he waiting for? It was time for God's vengeance on his enemies!

As it turns out, there was a twist in the story that even the prophets had not pieced together. For there was a day of judgment, of darkness, of earthquakes, of wrath being poured out on sin. Yet this was not carried out *by* Jesus Christ but *on* Jesus Christ. On the cross he bore the end-times punishment for the sins of his people. And in his rising he inaugurated the resurrection from the dead. These were end-times events taking place in the middle of human history.

So yet again, after his resurrection, the disciples were ready for Jesus to fulfill the day of the LORD: "Lord, will you at this time restore the kingdom to Israel?" (Acts 1:6). Jesus told them that it wasn't theirs to know and commanded them to bear witness to his resurrection to the ends of the earth. As Jesus ascended to his Father, two angels promised the disciples, "This Jesus, who was taken up from you into heaven, will come in the same way as you saw him go into heaven" (Acts 1:11). The day still lay ahead.

The Day of the Lord

This sets up one of the most profound reveals of how God's ancient promises would be fulfilled in the coming of his Son. For Jesus' disciples—steeped in Old Testament expectation and the teaching of their Lord—the promise of Jesus' return merged with their anticipation of the day of the LORD. This conflation appears in the subtle but significant shift in language from the "day of the LORD" to the "day of the Lord." Since for English readers that merely looks like the difference of a pressed Caps Lock key, let me unpack the dramatic distinction between those phrases.

When, hundreds of years before Jesus' birth, Jewish people ceased speaking the name Yahweh or YHWH in public worship out of reverence, they replaced it with Adonai, which means "Lord" or "Master." In their translation of the Old Testament into Greek, instances of YHWH were replaced with the Greek word *kurios*, which, like *adonai*, means lord or master. So our English shift from "the day of the LORD" to "the day of the Lord" represents a shift from "the day of YHWH" (OT Hebrew) to "the day of kurios" (OT Greek translation). The latter was picked up by the New Testament authors in referring to the day of Jesus' coming.

The significance of this is difficult to overstate. It equates Jesus with Yahweh, asserting that the return of Christ *is* the day of which the prophets spoke. When we anticipate Jesus' return, we stand in the same stream of hope that carried Isaiah and Jeremiah, Joel and Amos through times of idolatry and injustice. We connect to something as ancient as it is potent—the promise that God will repair what we have broken, in person. The New Testament contains at least twenty-five references to this day when Jesus will return to bring this about, with details that are no less epic than what the writing prophets foretold: "But the day of the Lord will come like a thief, and then the heavens will pass away with a roar, and the heavenly bodies will be burned up and dissolved, and the earth and the works that are done on it will be exposed" (2 Peter 3:10).

What Should We Expect?

The author of Hebrews captures the dynamic of this awesome and glorious day by relating it to Mount Sinai in Exodus 19. "For you have not come to what may be touched, a blazing fire and darkness and gloom and a tempest and the sound of a trumpet and a voice whose words made the hearers beg that no further messages be spoken to them" (Heb. 12:18–19). Rather, he writes, we who trust in Christ have come to a different mountain—Mount Zion, the heavenly Jerusalem, where we will dwell in the presence of God with the people of God. All of this was made possible by "Jesus, the mediator of a new covenant" and his blood shed for us (vv. 22–24).

The difference between these two mountains is not the fierceness of God's holiness or the weight of his glory. Indeed, the author goes on to quote Deuteronomy, that "our God is a consuming fire" (v. 29). No, the difference is that our experience of the presence of God will be a mediated experience because of "Jesus, the mediator."

Let me explain what I mean by a mediated experience. No human can go into space in shorts and a T-shirt and live. No human can swim a thousand feet underwater in only a bathing suit and live. The human body can't handle those environments unaided. And in the same way, as God told Moses on Mount Sinai, "you cannot see my face, for man shall not see me and live" (Ex. 33:20). But we can have a mediated experience of these environments. Astronauts can walk—or even swing a golf club—on the moon because of a space suit. A deep-sea diver can explore ocean depths, seeing manta rays, seahorses, and coral reefs because of the dive gear. In the same way, we will worship the Consuming Fire "with reverence and awe" (Heb. 12:28) because Christ mediates our experience of God through his death on our behalf.

So we anticipate this day with trembling hope and confidence in Christ alone. We will behold the Consuming Fire without being burned. We will hear the thunderous voice of God and beg to hear more, not less. We will dance on the mountain in the presence of God, all because of Christ our mediator.

Think about this through the experience of Robert Strank, William Kline, or the thief in South Africa that we met at the beginning of the chapter. Like each of them, we can eagerly await the coming rescue to release us from sickness and bondage. But that anticipation of rescue does not have to be mingled with dread of what the Enforcer will do when he comes. Because of Jesus' death on our behalf, believers have no outstanding warrants, no crimes waiting to be prosecuted. This should not elicit a glib "nothing to worry about" nonchalance about the day of the Lord. Rather, our posture should be one of profound reverence and gratitude that the one coming in judgment has already borne our judgment for us.

As we will explore in later chapters, a life focused on this final day transforms how we live today. We can resist the passing allurements of this age as we anticipate the superior satisfaction of experiencing this divine manifestation. We can view present afflictions against the backdrop of this final reckoning, knowing that no one has power over our final destiny but Jesus. And we can warn those still under Jesus' wrath to trust in him before it is too late, that they might experience the day of the Lord with delight, not dread.

May your today be shaped by your awe-filled hope in the day when Jesus returns.

Questions for Reflection

1. The Bible portrays both a holy, wrathful, and sovereign God and a loving, merciful, and near God. Do you tend to focus on one set of attributes over another?

2. Is there any aspect of God's holiness, wrath, or sovereignty that you struggle with? If so, why do you think that is?

3. Our hope is in the fact that God's judgment on our sin has already been poured out on Christ at the cross. Describe the emotional responses this stirs in your heart as you think about the coming day of the Lord.

4. Think through the overview of your life—relationships, work, church involvement, how you spend money and free time, and so on. Choose one of these and ask God how anticipating the day of the Lord should transform that area of your life.

CHAPTER 3

THE LORD'S APPEARINGS

I popped the question over lunch at Cracker Barrel. I didn't ask Rachael to marry me—I had asked that a few months earlier—but I asked whether she was open to the idea of adopting children. I had been part of a church that emphasized adoption as a meaningful way to pursue justice and mercy and wanted to hear her perspective. As our conversation meandered through preexisting expectations and new possibilities, we penciled down our agreement that we would think about adoption after we'd had a few children by birth.

Fast-forward past our wedding. After many fruitless months and futile doctors' visits, we decided to switch the order. We would pursue adoption now.

Adoption is an experience all its own. Many couples get pregnant apart from thoughtful planning. No one adopts a baby apart from thoughtful planning. The sheer amount of paperwork is so daunting that Rachael asked me to complete the thirty-four-page application as my gift to her for our second anniversary. You make excruciating decisions about what you are comfortable with in the child you might adopt—health issues, family history, ethnicity, and the birthparents' desire for an ongoing relationship. Everyone goes into parenting unaware of all that awaits them. The fact that adoption involves two families, not one, made us feel doubly unaware.

Let me pause the story for a moment at this sensation of being in the dark, not knowing what to expect. This is the experience we all bring to the issue of Jesus' appearing. One of the reasons we don't think about the Lord's coming more is because it is so foreign to us. We spend our days with humans who are not God incarnate. We have seen glimpses of the sublime in this sunset or that mountain view, but we have never seen the unveiled glory of the uncreated Creator. What will it be like? What could we even compare it to? How do we wrap our minds around anticipating this moment when we will see Jesus face to face?

Rachael and I attempted to compensate for our ignorance by reaching out to people who had been there. Rachael is a researcher by nature, so she immersed herself in adoption literature. We attended a weekend-long adoption seminar. We talked over many pots of coffee with adoptive couples in our church. Our adoption agency in Phoenix required us to attend a seven-week class in which we heard the stories of birthmothers, adoptive parents, and adopted children. The preparation was like a part-time job, but it familiarized us with what we could expect and prepared us for the experiences that lay ahead.

But what about Jesus' appearing in glory? How do we get our bearings on what to expect? Is there anyone we can talk to about what it is like to see Jesus in his resurrected splendor?

As it turns out, there is.

The Men Who Were There

While Jesus' final return is a future event no one has yet experienced, the New Testament contains accounts of Jesus' glorified appearings that give us hints of what the big reveal will be like. In fact, most of the men who called the church to set our hope on Jesus' revealing saw his glory revealed. Through their encounters we can pull up a chair, sit down with rapt attention, and ask, "What was it like?" to inform our own anticipation of seeing him face to face.

Peter writes about his experience on the Mount of Transfiguration with awe and delight—"For we did not follow cleverly devised myths when we made known to you the power and coming of our Lord Jesus Christ, but we were eyewitnesses of his majesty" (2 Peter 1:16). The word Peter uses for "coming" is the Greek word *parousia*, one of the three major words used for Christ's return (the other two are *apokalupsis*, "revelation," and *epiphaneia*, "appearing"). The basic meaning of *parousia* is "presence." This should not surprise us, after seeing in the previous chapter that the day of the Lord is the coming of God's presence. What Peter remembered years later was beholding the majesty of Jesus' presence.

Peter continues, "For when he received honor and glory from God the Father, and the voice was borne to him by the Majestic Glory, 'This is my beloved Son, with whom I am well pleased,' we ourselves heard this very voice borne from heaven, for we were with him on the holy mountain" (vv. 17–18).

So when Peter calls us to "hope fully" in Christ's return (1 Peter 1:13) or asks "what sort of people ought you to be"

(2 Peter 3:11) in anticipation of the day of the Lord, he is not writing theoretically. He has seen as much of Christ's glory as unglorified human eyes can behold. His experience gives confirmation to "the prophetic word" about Jesus' end-times appearing, "to which you will do well to pay attention as to a lamp shining in a dark place, until the day dawns and the morning star rises in your hearts" (2 Peter 1:19).

So let's pull up a chair, put on a pot of coffee, and ask "What was it like?" to the men who saw the Lord's appearings in person, in order to give more definition to our own question of "What will it be like?" We will begin with the Mount of Transfiguration, where Peter, James, and John were present with the glorified Jesus, then note the similar themes in Paul's Damascus Road encounter and John's vision of the glorified Christ on Patmos.

The Mount of Transfiguration

In each of the gospel accounts,[16] the Mount of Transfiguration is prefaced by Jesus' statement that "there are some standing here who will not taste death until they see the kingdom of God after it has come with power" (Mark 9:1). Peter, James, and John had to wait only about a week to find out what Jesus was talking about. What began as a typical prayer getaway turned into a once-in-a-lifetime glimpse of Jesus' divine glory.

The entire account echoes God's powerful appearance on Mount Sinai, which we studied in the previous chapter from Exodus 19. Beyond the obvious fact that both accounts involve a mountain, they also include a thick cloud, a thundering voice, brilliant flashes, and great fear on the part of those observing the glory.

Only the glory that Peter, James, and John beheld was not of a storm brewing far off at the top of the mountain. They walked up the mountain and watched as their teacher, traveling companion, and friend was changed—transfigured—to reveal more and more of his true, brilliant nature. The gospel writers exhaust the limits of language to describe the unveiled radiance of Jesus, God the eternal Son.

"His face shone like the sun," Matthew writes (17:2). Think about that for a moment. Certainly many of us have broken our mother's rule and caught a direct glimpse of the sun. But you can't look long, and when you look away, all you see is the imprint of that overwhelming splendor. Imagine the brightness level of Jesus' presumably cheerful countenance being dialed up to "Sunshine." Imagine wanting to look away but not being able to, even as this radiance is burning into your corneas. Imagine wondering, "Who *is* this?" as not only his face is transfigured but "his clothes became radiant, intensely white, as no one on earth could bleach them" (Mark 9:3).

This was an upgrade from Israel's experience at Sinai. There they saw a shining face when Moses came down from the mountain. But this was different. As one commentator states it, "Moses shone for a time with a reflection of the divine glory he had seen; Jesus shone with his own heavenly glory. Moses' radiance was derivative, Jesus' essential."[17]

Now is the part of the story where we ask Peter, James, and John, "What was it like?" The text gives two reactions.

First, they were terrified. They fell on their faces at the sound of God's "this is my beloved Son" declaration. They feared the thick cloud that overshadowed them. The whole experience left them scared out of their minds.

Second, they wanted the experience to last forever. This is my understanding of what Peter was after when he suggested, "Master, it is good that we are here. Let us make three tents, one for you and one for Moses and one for Elijah" (Luke 9:33). The text makes clear that Peter didn't know what he was saying for the terror of the experience. (See reaction 1.) But even being out of his mind with fear, Peter characteristically voiced his instinct. He didn't want the episode to end. Rather, "Peter wants to freeze the moment. . . . This is Peter's version of the beatific vision and he does not want it to go away!"[18]

This would not make sense if the encounter were only sheer terror for the disciples. But Jesus' words suggest that their initial fear at the power and presence of the Almighty would give way to something more sustainable. Matthew records that Jesus came to the facedown disciples "and touched them, saying, 'Rise, and have no fear'" (Matt. 17:7). Certainly the words of the author of Hebrews describe the type of ongoing experience the disciples could have: "Let us offer to God acceptable worship, with reverence and awe, for our God is a consuming fire" (Heb. 12:28–29).

Even the presence of Moses and Elijah on the mountain provides encouragement that such a day of unending worship will come. The only time these two characters are mentioned together before this event is at the end of the Old Testament. The prophet Malachi warns about the day of judgment that will set ablaze the wicked but will signal light and release for God's people: "The sun of righteousness shall rise with healing in its wings" (Mal. 4:2). Then he calls them to "remember the law of my servant Moses" and promises "behold, I will send you Elijah the prophet before the great and awesome day of the LORD comes" (vv. 4–5).

Fast-forward to the Mount of Transfiguration, and there Moses and Elijah stand, side by side with the Sun of righteousness, the Healer, the one who would bring that final day about. Peter's desire to freeze the moment may not be granted now, but he can rest assured that such a day will come. Jesus, who alone remains once Moses and Elijah are gone, will fulfill all the hopes they represent.

Damascus and Patmos

The experiences of Paul on the road to Damascus and John on the island of Patmos bear striking similarities to Jesus' appearance on the Mount of Transfiguration. Paul (then Saul) was blinded by the light that shone on him when the risen Christ stopped him in his tracks. Later he described this light from heaven as "brighter than the sun" (Acts 26:13). The brilliance so stunned him that "for three days he was without sight, and neither ate nor drank" (Acts 9:9).

This glorious appearance was so significant to Paul's theology and mission that Luke, the author of Acts and Paul's traveling companion, records it three times. The Lord's self-identification, "I am Jesus, whom you are persecuting" (9:5), introduced Paul to the deep, spiritual union between Christ and his church. Paul knew that he was persecuting Jesus' followers, so the Savior's question, "Why are you persecuting me?" (v. 4) highlights Jesus' solidarity with his own and plants "the roots of the concept of 'the body of Christ.'"[19]

Likewise, Jesus' glorious appearing to Paul launched his mission to the gentiles. The voice booming out of the blinding light told Paul, "I have appeared to you for this purpose, to appoint you as a servant and a witness of what you have seen and will see of me. I will rescue you from your people and from the Gentiles. I am sending you to them" (Acts 26:16–17 CSB). This mission came with a cost, as Jesus also communicated to Paul "how much he must suffer for the sake of my name" (9:16).

Yet the glory made it worth the pain. Throughout Paul's letters he places his considerable suffering for Christ against the backdrop of the glory of Christ. He continued not because the insults didn't sting, not because the lashes didn't leave scars, not because the betrayal wasn't excruciating but because Christ was his all. The vision of Jesus' resurrection glory ("what you have seen . . . of me") was meant to sustain Paul. And in that singular moment when he would see the glory again ("what you . . . will see of me"), Paul knew it would be worth it.

John's Revelation opens with a vision that describes a similar light, only more specifically connected to Jesus' resurrected appearance. John describes this "one like a son of man": "The hairs of his head were white, like white wool, like snow. His eyes were like a flame of fire, his feet were like burnished bronze, refined in a furnace, and his voice was like the roar of many waters. In his right hand he held seven stars, from his mouth came a sharp two-edged sword, and his face was like the sun shining in full strength" (Rev. 1:13–16).

Not surprisingly, at this sight John "fell at his feet as though dead." Yet, just as on the Mount of Transfiguration, Jesus "laid his right hand on me, saying, 'Fear not, I am the first and the last, and the living one. I died, and behold I am alive forevermore, and I have the keys of Death and Hades'" (vv. 17–18).

Like Paul's, John's vision of his resurrected Lord in unveiled splendor took place in the context of suffering. He wrote to the seven churches of Asia as a "partner in the tribulation . . . on the island called Patmos on account of the word of God and the testimony of Jesus" (Rev. 1:9). The vision of Jesus' appearing he was granted was not for him alone but also for the churches. Each letter that Jesus dictates to him opens with a snippet from the glorious vision of the Son of Man. In these letters, Jesus calls his followers to faithful endurance, even to the death. He calls them to purity of life and doctrine. He calls them to separate themselves from the idolatrous celebrations in their communities, even though it will cost them financially and socially. But it will be worth it because of who Jesus Christ is in his bright beauty. It will be worth it because all who trust in him will be enveloped in this glory not for a few brief moments but for eternity.

An Invitation to Beauty and Mystery

The lives of Peter, Paul, and John model a sweet spot of being grounded in present ministry while longing to see the splendor of Jesus again. They didn't spend their days chasing their first spiritual high or telling the same glory story over and over. They were invested in the real lives of suffering people and endured patiently the hardships associated with faithful witness to Jesus, whether from Jews who were not convinced that Jesus was the Messiah or gentiles who luxuriated in debauchery and ridiculed the idea of resurrection. Their example is an invitation to us to prioritize meditation on the beauty of Christ in the midst of ministry and its inevitable seasons of difficulty.

We are conditioned to view beauty as nonessential, whether it is the arts, breathtaking vistas in nature, or our simple, daily focus on the virtuous over the vicious. We think of these as luxuries. Yet Scripture identifies the beholding of divine beauty as essential to faithfulness in ministry. Yahweh disclosed a vision of his heavenly brilliance to Isaiah (Isa. 6:1–6) and Ezekiel (Ezekiel 1–3) to sustain them through the challenges of their ministry. King David was sustained through the trials of being hunted by Saul and reigning over Israel by the "one thing" he asked of God: "to gaze upon the beauty of the LORD" (Ps. 27:4). And as we have seen in this chapter, Jesus unveiled his royal splendor to the ones he knew would face tremendous hardship in spreading his gospel.

Will you respond to this invitation to prioritize meditation on the beauty of Christ? As you commit to investing your resources in the lives of others so that they might know Christ, pay attention to how much time you need to spend delighting in Jesus' magnificence to counterbalance the ugliness of sin—both theirs and yours—that ministry exposes. Make the appearings of Jesus that we have explored in this chapter and the portraits of his return we will unpack in the next section the focus of your attention. Give yourself permission to upgrade this practice to "essential" status. And if you wonder when you will find the time to do this, bring this discipline of seeing beauty into how you read part 3 as you include gathering, fasting, and resting into your weekly rhythms.

Dr. Diane Langberg, a psychologist who has walked with survivors of abuse for more than thirty-five years, identifies this necessity of prioritizing beauty. As she hears the stories of horrific evils abusers have perpetrated, she is aware that "if I am to endure and not get twisted by the darkness . . . [I] must pursue the antidote for the poison I encounter in this world. That antidote is beauty." She finds that beauty in "the natural world, in music, in good friends, and in family" as well as in drawing near to God. These pursuits "nourish and replenish me as I continue on with this work grounded in hope."[20]

At the same time that beholding divine beauty enables us to endure, we will always live our days leaning into the mystery of what lies ahead. Rachael and I discovered this when the day came for us to meet our first child. As thorough as our adoption training was, there was one particular moment that nothing could have prepared us for. When our daughter Sophia was born, her birthmother invited us to visit them in the hospital. The experience of meeting our daughter, her birthmother, and her family for the first time was suffused with emotion. So much was going on in the room as we worked through introductions, aware of the lifetime of commitment represented in this gathering.

The next day, Sophia's birthmother was released from the hospital a few hours before Sophia, so we needed to be there to hold our new baby in the hospital room before we could take her home. The moment that nothing could have prepared us for was when Sophia's birthmother handed her to Rachael. After a few last expressions of "I love you," all felt silent. All the grieving and courage and resolve and finality hung in the air, palpable. And all that remained to do was weep. As she handed her newborn to my wife, Sophia's birthmother wept. Her mother wept. Rachael and I wept. The nurse wept. The only person not in a mess of tears in that moment was Sophia, sleeping serenely, surrounded by love.

Words could never fully communicate the profound poignancy of that moment. It remains indelibly etched on our hearts. You can imagine it and may even tear up with me as I recall it. But there is no substitute for experiencing that holy moment of love.

I pray that you will be energized by the awareness that all the meditation on Jesus' beauty by faith—sustaining as it is—will never fully prepare you for being in the blazing presence of his holy love. In the moment when he appears, faith will become sight. The partial will give way to the perfect. Every doubt will melt away. In the presence of the Son of God, "who loved me and gave himself for me" (Gal. 2:20), you will never want to leave. And you will never have to, because "we will always be with the Lord" (1 Thess. 4:17).

Questions for Reflection

1. What have you seen in the physical creation that was so brilliant and beautiful it nearly terrified you? As you recall that experience, what other emotions did you feel when you beheld it?

2. Read slowly through the Mount of Transfiguration account in Matthew 17:1–7. (It also appears in Mark 9:2–10 and Luke 9:28–36 if you want a fuller read.) Imagine yourself with Jesus on the mountain. Describe what you experience as you behold Jesus in his unveiled glory.

3. What event, encounter, or experience are you looking forward to the most in the next six months? Without minimizing its importance, how does it compare in splendor when set against the glory of Jesus on the Mount of Transfiguration? Rather than distracting from Jesus' appearing, how might your six-month anticipation help point you toward this ultimate hope?

4. What do you fear the most as you look to the next six months? How will seeing Jesus embolden you to say, "It was worth it"?

5. As you meditate on the following words, ask the Holy Spirit to help you feel and hear the assurance of Jesus that he gave to those who saw his glory.

   - "But Jesus came and touched them, saying, 'Rise, and have no fear'" (Matt. 17:7).
   - "When I saw him, I fell at his feet as though dead. But he laid his right hand on me, saying, 'Fear not, I am the first and the last'" (Rev. 1:17).

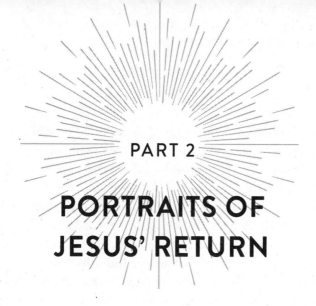

PART 2

PORTRAITS OF JESUS' RETURN

What will we see when we behold Christ at his appearing? Jesus' return is such a robust event that no single metaphor or image can capture it. The New Testament speaks of Jesus as the Warrior King bringing vengeance on his enemies, the Bridegroom coming for his bride, the Judge whose assessment alone matters to the eternal joy of his people, and the Resurrecting One who returns to this deteriorating world to make all things new. We will look at each of these portraits in depth over the next four chapters.

These portraits fill out not only the richness of Christ's return but also the variety of his people's needs. If you are experiencing physical illness but are not facing persecution or injustice, you might gravitate toward focusing on Jesus' return as the Resurrecting One over his coming as Warrior King. They are both equally true, but some aspects of Jesus' appearing will stand out more at certain times. As we will see, the portrait Paul or Peter or John paints often responds to the context they were writing into, and context continues to matter today.

Pay attention to the nature of these descriptions of Jesus' return as portraits. You are meant to see Jesus coming with the eyes of faith. "Christian hope . . . is not imaginary, but it is irreducibly imaginative."[21] As the Psalms, Prophets, and Revelation bear out, God seems to engage his people more imaginatively in times of increased persecution, temptation, and affliction. Visions of the Shepherd, the enthroned King, or the Lion of Judah fuel endurance through these times. In the same way, these portraits of Jesus' appearing can enliven your faith. Ask the Spirit to grant you an active imagination and an emotional engagement with this gallery of hope.

CHAPTER 4

THE WARRIOR KING

The first portrait of Jesus' appearing we will view is one that may feel puzzling, even irrelevant to many American Christians. So let's take a moment to zoom out from our personal and historical situations to consider what followers of Jesus face in different parts of the world.

One of my living heroes is a woman in India whose name I do not know. I have never met her and likely will not this side of Jesus' return. But a number of years ago I had the privilege of watching a video in which she shared her story of persecution, a story that I hope will make some sense out of why we are focusing on Jesus' coming as Warrior King.[22]

In 2014, a Hindu extremist group showed up to her village in northern India on a Saturday and announced near the church building, "If anyone comes to worship here tomorrow, we will beat them, and all the things they have will be taken." Many were understandably frightened by this and fled to a nearby large city, where the pastor of their mother church gave them shelter. But others decided that they would stay and worship, whatever the cost.

The next day came and the church members gathered, singing praises to God. What they didn't realize is that the extremist group had been recruiting in the surrounding villages and brought a large mob with them. The group descended on the congregants during their Sunday worship service, yelling insults, tearing up Bibles, and using large bamboo sticks to beat men and women alike.

The worshipers scattered. When the woman in the video sought refuge inside her home, the mob threw large stones on the corrugated roof until it collapsed. Gaining entrance, they beat her with the sticks, smashed every possession, great and small, and stole her legal documents and life's savings. As she tried to crawl away from them, they continued to beat her. All she could do is cry out, "Lord Jesus, save me!"

Longing for the Warrior King

Linger over the Indian sister's words: "Lord Jesus, save me!"

The salvation Jesus brings is multifaceted. Jesus saves us from the spiritual powers of sin, Satan, and eternal death through his crucifixion. He saves us from the deterioration of our bodies and minds through his resurrection, giving us healing in this life and raising us with a body like his in the life to come. And Jesus saves his people from persecution. Like healing, sometimes he brings this about in this life, and sometimes he calls his own to follow him all the way to death. But his final rescue is sure, and his people can cry out, "Lord Jesus, save me!" because "Christ, having been offered once to bear the sins of many, will appear a second time, not to deal with sin but to save those who are eagerly waiting for him" (Heb. 9:28).

While we can see this holistic salvation now, at the time of Jesus' first appearing, those languishing under Roman oppression were not so sure. John the Baptist, who prepared the way for Jesus' public ministry, sent messengers from prison to ask, "Are you the one who is to come, or shall we look for another?" (Luke 7:19). John had pronounced in Jesus the coming of "the salvation of God" that would include wrath, fire, and an axe laid to the root (Luke 3:4–9). Now John was in prison, decidedly unrescued, and wondered whether he had identified the wrong one as Messiah. From James and John requesting to sit on thrones flanking Jesus "in your glory" (Mark 10:37) to Peter rebuking Jesus' insinuation of crucifixion and slashing his sword at the soldiers arresting his Master, this question of Jesus' relationship to the Roman and Jewish power structures of his day sits tensely in the backdrop of all the gospel narratives.

We anticipate Jesus' second coming in a similar way to how John the Baptist and others anticipated his first. He will return not as the sacrificial lamb or the suffering servant but as the Warrior King. We share their ancient hope of rescue: his real promise to deal with the real aggressors who harm us. While we will focus on the immediate context of persecution for the faith, I believe the imagery of deliverance could help you who have suffered abuse, discrimination, or harassment. These are tragically prevalent in our day, and if they are part of your story, I pray you will find hope in beholding this aspect of Jesus.

The *Thlipsis* of the Thessalonians

The apostle Paul ministered under constant persecution, receiving the same dogged aggression from Jewish religious leaders that he once carried out against Jesus' followers. This was not hidden in the fine print of his conversion. Days after Paul's blinding Damascus road encounter, Jesus sent word to him by a messenger: "I will show him how much he must suffer for the sake of my name" (Acts 9:16).

Paul spoke openly of this expectation of persecution for Jesus' sake wherever he shared the gospel. One of the places where new converts faced fierce, immediate opposition was in Thessalonica. Indeed, because of public outcry Paul was able to proclaim the news about Jesus for only three weeks before he was forced out of the city (Acts 17:1–9). Not long after, he wrote to the brand-new church about the persecution they continued to face.

In both of his letters, Paul speaks often about their "afflictions" (*thlipsis* in the Greek) because of their allegiance to Christ. When they first believed, the Thessalonians "received the word in much affliction" (1 Thess. 1:6). After his expulsion from the city, Paul sent Timothy back to exhort the new, persecuted believers "that no one be moved by these afflictions" (1 Thess. 3:3). He rejoiced upon learning from Timothy that "you are standing fast in the Lord" (v. 8).

Whatever time passed between Paul's first and second letters to the Thessalonians, the afflictions did not abate. The young church had persevered so admirably that Paul wrote, "We ourselves boast about you in the churches of God for your steadfastness and faith in all your persecutions and in the afflictions that you are enduring" (2 Thess. 1:4). Apparently the church misunderstood Paul's teaching on Jesus' return—a confusion complicated by a letter, falsely attributed to Paul, teaching that "the day of the Lord has come" (2:2). So Paul merges the issues of their afflictions and the day of the Lord to explain exactly what will happen when their Savior appears. He holds out to them the hope of rescue.

The Warrior King

We do not know the precise nature of the Thessalonians' persecution. Acts 17:5 records an attack on the house of Jason during Paul's ministry in Thessalonica that sounds similar to what our sister in India endured—physical beating and the destruction of property by an angry mob. Their experience of *thlipsis* likely also included social and economic ostracization and an unwillingness of the government to protect them from acts of aggression.

The larger story of these afflictions is the story of powerlessness. Abuse survivors have tasted it. Victims of workplace discrimination know it. Anyone who has been on the wrong end of the misuse of power has felt helplessness to stop what is being done or to find justice when the aggressor is protected. Having no voice, no recourse, no traction with your account of what happened is one of the most horrific and dehumanizing experiences in this fallen world.

With that taste of powerlessness in your mouth, consider

the hope you would feel when you beheld this vision of Jesus: "God considers it just to repay with affliction those who afflict you, and to grant relief to you who are afflicted as well as to us, when the Lord Jesus is revealed from heaven with his mighty angels in flaming fire, inflicting vengeance on those who do not know God and on those who do not obey the gospel of our Lord Jesus" (2 Thess. 1:6–8).

Let's use our sanctified imagination to develop this portrait of Jesus' appearing as Warrior King. I'm going to suggest a thought experiment that will be immediately applicable for some and something to file away for others. If you are facing affliction, my guess is that the person or group that is making you miserable looms large over your life, haunting your thoughts. I wish there were a way to erase their image from the canvas of your mind. I'm not sure there is. But there is a way to paint something around that image that will put the terrible afflictions you face now into a larger context.

Paul says that Jesus will come "with his mighty angels." This is not the first reference connecting Jesus with an army of angels. On the night of his betrayal, Jesus commanded Peter to put his sword away because, had Jesus needed military backup, he could call on his Father and "he will at once send me more than twelve legions of angels" (Matt. 26:53). A Roman legion consisted of six thousand soldiers. Whether Jesus meant exactly 72,000 angels or simply an innumerable host, the point is that they serve to fight at his command. Of course, he doesn't need them, being God the Son, almighty and eternal. But the optics give a stunning visual for those overwhelmed by persecution.

So on the canvas of your mind, where you see the menacing face of the one antagonizing you, imagine behind them the risen Christ. Surrounding him are thousands of angels. If you're trying to mentally populate the space, imagine a line of thirty-six angel warriors on either side of Jesus, backfilled a thousand warriors deep, as far as your eye can see.

But don't forget the fire. Jesus is portrayed "in flaming fire," a common theme in most visions of the risen Jesus and a symbol of judgment and purification throughout the Bible. So however you were envisioning Jesus before on your mental canvas, this one is not cuddling a lamb or smiling serenely toward heaven. This Jesus is on the move, forward marching, sword in hand, blazing with the fiery judgment of God, coming to bring relief to you and to inflict vengeance on those who torment you. Help is on the way.

Be Faithful unto Death

Of course, nothing Paul says promises deliverance in this life.[23] Jesus' vengeful return would mean fiery judgment for those causing the afflictions, but that may not happen until the age to come. Indeed, in Jesus' letter to the church in Smyrna, he acknowledges their tribulation and commands them, "Be faithful unto death, and I will give you the crown of life" (Rev. 2:10). Their reward will not come until after their martyrdom.

So the vision of the Warrior King is not given for us to claim immediate, temporal deliverance from our opponents. Yet in a very real way, it bolsters the cry of the afflicted,

"Lord Jesus, save me!" Those in Smyrna who kept listening to John's Revelation beyond their ominous message heard a further word about the end their persecutors would meet:

> Then I saw heaven opened, and behold, a white horse! The one sitting on it is called Faithful and True, and in righteousness he judges and makes war. His eyes are like a flame of fire, and on his head are many diadems, and he has a name written that no one knows but himself. He is clothed in a robe dipped in blood, and the name by which he is called is The Word of God. And the armies of heaven, arrayed in fine linen, white and pure, were following him on white horses. From his mouth comes a sharp sword with which to strike down the nations, and he will rule them with a rod of iron. He will tread the winepress of the fury of the wrath of God the Almighty. On his robe and on his thigh he has a name written, King of kings and Lord of lords.
>
> —Revelation 19:11–16

This vision is what empowers the endurance of the afflicted. Whenever he chooses to deliver us, Jesus is our Savior.

When we walk by faith in this vision of Jesus, rather than by sight in our circumstances, we stand in a long and beautiful tradition. Hebrews 11:27 says that Moses wasn't afraid of Pharaoh's anger, "for he endured as seeing him who is invisible." This is remarkable when you consider how powerful Pharaoh was. There's a similar story involving the prophet

Elisha. When the king of Syria sent "horses and chariots and a great army" (2 Kings 6:14) to seize Elisha, there was something to be seen by sight, and when Elisha's servant saw this great horde, he was understandably terrified. Then Elisha prayed for his eyes to be opened, "and behold, the mountain was full of horses and chariots of fire all around Elisha" (v. 17), giving credence to Elisha's words to his servant, "Do not be afraid, for those who are with us are more than those who are with them" (v. 16).

Our eyes never see the whole picture. The power, wealth, acclaim, and popularity we see around us are often mirages and always fleeting. What is real is that which is unseen. As Paul writes in 2 Corinthians 4:18, "We look not to the things that are seen but to the things that are unseen. For the things that are seen are transient, but the things that are unseen are eternal." This was one of the key verses that a family in our church in Phoenix held onto as the father walked through years of treating the cancer that finally took his life. They knew the cancer was real and death was real. But there was something more real, and they chose to walk by faith in the conquering power of Jesus, even to death.

Doubtless you have an area in your life where you hear the call to walk by faith in Jesus' promise to rescue rather than succumbing to despair. Whether your small business faces tumultuous market changes, your local government threatens your civil liberties, or a drug epidemic sweeps family members into its vortex, you can walk through these terrifying times with the hope that Jesus will bring about your final deliverance.

"Save Me!"

The sister in India who was beaten and robbed for her allegiance to Jesus is one of my living heroes because of what she reported was going through her mind during the attack. She said, "I felt, to live is Christ and to die is gain. And even if I am beaten it is all joy. Those of us who were beaten are the privileged ones. So we live for Christ, and when we die, we die for Christ. We have completely given our lives into the hand of Jesus."[24]

Through the Spirit's work in our hearts, afflictions can cause us to cry out, "Lord Jesus, save me!" They draw us close to the Savior, who alone will bring about final justice in the end. And his sure vengeance gives us the freedom not to be a people of vengeance, of violence against our enemies. Rather, it frees us to love our enemies and pray that they too would be saved by Jesus. This is not a blanket call to race back to your abuser in a way that would make you susceptible to more harm.[25] But when the afflictions or the memories of what you endured rear their ugly heads, you can pray for the faith to see this vision of Jesus "with his mighty angels in flaming fire, inflicting vengeance" and to know that he will bring about a perfect justice, one you could never execute. And perhaps as you focus on this portrait, the vision of the one who brought you affliction "suffer[ing] the punishment of eternal destruction, away from the presence of the Lord" (2 Thess. 1:9) will impel you to pray for them to repent before it is too late, expanding your "Lord Jesus, save me!" to "Lord Jesus, save us!"

Questions for Reflection

1. Is the image of Jesus as Warrior King congruent with or at odds with the understanding of Jesus you had coming into this chapter? How do you understand his justice to relate to his mercy and kindness?

2. What afflictions or opposition have you faced from others, whether in general or for your allegiance to Jesus?

3. How do you typically respond to those afflictions? You could include emotional or physical responses, habits you turn to (healthy or unhealthy), and the kind of support you receive from others.

4. Now work through the thought experiment on pages 60–61. How does this experiment transform how you view those who have harmed you? What do you feel at the thought of standing before such a King?

5. While there are some ways in which you have experienced powerlessness, there are other ways in which you have power now. What next step is God calling you to take—pursuing legal action, sharing your story with others, advocating for the afflicted, or some other proactive step?

CHAPTER 5

THE BRIDEGROOM

I will never forget the flight from Minneapolis to Atlanta on December 18, 2003. A year earlier my friendship with Rachael Nobles, marked by long emails about theological issues and ministry opportunities, had transformed into a dizzying euphoria of attraction and yearning to always be together. And now, a year to the day after our first date, when I fell in love with Rachael, I was going to marry her. There was a lot going on that week—I had just taken my final exams at seminary and watched the midnight premier of the final installment of the Lord of the Rings trilogy, the movie of the year for Tolkien nerds like me. But these significant events fell into the background of my longing to finally be married. No more going to separate apartments at the end of dinner. No more disconnect between desire and expression. The two were soon to become one and I could hardly contain the excitement.

With this memory of full hope so strong nearly two decades later, you would think the idea of anticipating Jesus' return as the Bridegroom would be the most accessible of all the portraits. But the metaphor doesn't click into place automatically. For starters, Rachael is a woman I knew in person, but Jesus is a man I read about in the pages of Scripture. The bride that says, "Come, Lord Jesus!" to her Bridegroom (Rev. 22:17, 20) is not an individual but a massive group of people, the church. Then the uncomfortable question: What is the spiritual equivalent of the physical union between a husband and wife that consummates their marriage?

Furthermore, while I am blessed with a marriage that has only increased in joy and intimacy, I don't know your story. Perhaps you long to be married but are not. Perhaps you thought you found your one true love but the relationship soured and led to divorce. Perhaps you had a beautiful marriage cut short by the death of your spouse. Perhaps you feel like your marriage is nothing to write home about. We bring to this spiritual topic a variety of experiences from the marriages we have been in and around, and those relationships are as painful for some as they are ecstatic for others.

Clearly there is a lot to unpack as we ask what it means for us as Christ's bride to long for his return as our Bridegroom. The explicit reference to this return appears at the end of the Bible, in Revelation 19:6–10 and 22:17. These passages anticipate the marriage supper of the Lamb and express the bride's longing for Christ's return. Yet this return is only referenced, not explained in detail. So we will expand our biblical survey to the whole story of God's marital relationship with his people in order to gain greater clarity on what we are anticipating.

This study will address two questions. First, what kind of

relationship is this between Jesus and his bride? Second, for what exactly are we waiting when we anticipate Jesus' return as Bridegroom? If we think of this second question in terms of a modern ceremony, is it the part of the wedding when the bride walks down the aisle to be presented to the groom? Or is it the part of the reception when the emcee introduces the new couple together? Or maybe after the festivities when the husband whisks his new bride away on a mighty steed—or at least in a rented limousine? On what part of this ceremony are we setting our expectation? Without spoiling anything, I can assure you that there is a plot twist near the end of this love story that you will not see coming.

What Kind of Relationship Is This?

Paul's treatment in Ephesians 5:22–33 of the marital relationship between Christ and the church, interwoven with his instructions to husbands and wives, is the most thorough in the New Testament. We will use that as our base camp for exploring what kind of relationship this is, taking excursions to other marriages in the Scriptures that Paul references.

A Relationship of Intimacy: Adam and Eve

After describing how Christ "nourishes and cherishes" the church (Eph. 5:29), Paul quotes from Genesis 2, about the first marriage in the Bible: "Therefore a man shall leave his father and mother and hold fast to his wife, and the two shall become one flesh" (Eph. 5:31). Let's begin there to see what kind of relationship we as the church have with our Bridegroom.

The story of marriage begins when the LORD God observed the only thing in all of his creation that was not good and announced what he had to do about it: "It is not good that the man should be alone; I will make him a helper fit for him" (Gen. 2:18). When God fashions the woman and brings her to Adam, we hear the first poem in the Bible:

> "This at last is bone of my bones
> and flesh of my flesh;
> she shall be called Woman,
> because she was taken out of Man."
>
> —verse 23

Then we read the gold standard of this covenantal relationship: "Therefore a man shall leave his father and his mother and hold fast to his wife, and they shall become one flesh. And the man and his wife were both naked and were not ashamed" (vv. 24–25).

Naked and not ashamed. Such are the depths of intimacy made possible in this union of two people. To be fully exposed, vulnerable, and known, yet entirely loved, welcomed, and cherished, is the apex of human joys. It is the image of God fully realized, as the loving communion of two reflects the eternal self-giving, luxuriating love of the Father and Son through the Spirit. It is relational paradise.

Paul writes that the mystery of two becoming one flesh "is profound, and I am saying that it refers to Christ and the church" (Eph. 5:32). Because of the sin that Adam and Eve committed in the chapter following their glorious marriage, the sin we both inherit and continue to commit, we come to our relationship with Jesus ashamed. When we stand naked before him, he sees our shame, the same shame that sent Adam and Eve hiding in the bushes and covering themselves with fig leaves. But Jesus does not turn away in disgust. Rather, he cleanses us so that we can stand before him both unashamed and fully embraced. To that we turn our attention next.

A Relationship of Faithfulness: Yahweh and Israel

Paul expresses this cleansing by saying of the church that Jesus "cleansed her by the washing of water with the word, so that he might present the church to himself in splendor, without spot or wrinkle or any such thing, that she might be holy and without blemish" (Eph. 5:26–27).

This washing recalls the relationship between Yahweh and Israel in the Old Testament, a relationship we must explore to fully appreciate the union between Christ and the church. Let's start from the beginning.

The marital love of Yahweh for his people was initiated in the promises he made to Abram to bless him with land and descendants and favor such that "in you all the families of the earth shall be blessed" (Gen. 12:3). From the beginning of this relationship, God made clear through his words and a "covenant cutting" ceremony (Genesis 15) that he would be faithful to his part of the covenant. In response, he called his people to the same faithfulness, beginning with the sign of circumcision (Genesis 17). The Hebrew word for this covenant faithfulness, *hesed*, is translated as steadfast love, faithful love, lovingkindness, or mercy. It describes one's loyalty to his or her promises, an absolute commitment to a covenant.

With this *hesed* at the center of God's relationship with his people, it should not surprise us that the prophets used marital language to describe God's covenant with Israel. Ezekiel delivers the word of Yahweh that compares Israel to an infant left to die in the wilderness. God not only brought her to life and provided for her, but when she was "at the age for love . . . I made my vow to you and entered into a covenant with you, declares the LORD GOD, and you became mine" (Ezek. 16:8). It is in this context that the prophet uses the washing language that Paul references in Ephesians 5: "I bathed you with water and washed off your blood from you and anointed you with oil" (Ezek. 16:9). The text goes on to describe the bride's elaborate adornment and increasing beauty. In Jeremiah, Yahweh describes Israel's eager agreement to obey his law as "the devotion of your youth, your love as a bride" (Jer. 2:2).

Sadly, this ideal beginning serves as a stark contrast to the unraveling of Israel's faithfulness to her Husband. Whether through idolatry—serving the gods of their neighbors out of a sense of Yahweh's inadequacy—or injustice—leveraging power to take from one another rather than trusting their Bridegroom's provision—God's people shamelessly broke their covenantal vows.

The prophets indict this faithlessness with language that might cause us to wince. In Ezekiel, Yahweh condemns Israel's "sick heart" with these gut-wrenching words: "Adulterous wife, who receives strangers instead of her husband! Men give gifts to all prostitutes, but you gave your gifts to all your lovers, bribing them to come to you from every side with your whorings" (Ezek. 16:30–33).

Most of Ezekiel 16 is difficult to read. God showed Israel nothing but *hesed*, completely undeserved. And in response she looked outside her covenant bond with him for pleasure and belonging. Perhaps with the low lights and mood music the adultery made sense. But the daylight reveals Israel's whoring for the disgusting treachery that it is. Ezekiel describes the spiritual adultery of Israel's idolatry in unrelenting detail, chronicling her trust in other nations and their gods rather than her true Lover.

This faithlessness is not confined to the Old Testament. Centuries later such betrayal by God's people is captured in James 4:3–4 as it relates to their prayers. "You ask and do not receive, because you ask wrongly, to spend it on your passions. You adulterous people! Do you not know that friendship with the world is enmity with God?"

This senseless instinct to reject the only one who truly shows us kindness and loyalty is the most pernicious effect of sin. How can this self-destructive trajectory end in anything but tragedy?

Because of God's fathomless mercy, this is not the end of the story. Ezekiel, after relaying the harrowing account of Israel's faithlessness and the consequences of her disobedience, ends chapter 16 with the hope of God's enduring faithfulness: "For thus says the Lord GOD: I will deal with you as you have done, you who have despised the oath in breaking the covenant, yet I will remember my covenant with you in the days of your youth, and I will establish for you an everlasting covenant. . . . And you shall know that I am the LORD, that you may remember and be confounded, and never open your mouth again because of your shame, when I atone for you for all that you have done, declares the Lord GOD" (Ezek. 16:59–60, 62–63).

Yahweh's radical love for his faithless bride is also powerfully conveyed by the life and prophecies of Hosea. God commands the prophet to marry an adulterous woman and to pursue her after her sexual unfaithfulness. This husband's bewildering pursuit of his disloyal wife portrays Yahweh's pursuit of his disobedient people. After her string of spiritual infidelities, God promises, "I will betroth you to me forever. I will betroth you to me in righteousness and in justice, in steadfast love [*hesed*] and in mercy. I will betroth you to me in faithfulness. And you shall know the LORD" (Hos. 2:19–20).

A Relationship of Sacrifice: Christ and the Church

This is gospel love—love that washes us from our filth and cleans us up so that we might be brought into a pure, blissful, secure, eternal relationship with our loving Redeemer. By borrowing from the language of Yahweh's staggering love for his people, Paul sets up the climax of that display of *hesed:* the cross of Christ. The cleansing of the church came at the greatest price. It was when "Christ loved the church and gave himself up for her" (Eph. 5:25) that he cleansed her. It was through his ultimate sacrifice that he was able to remove our sin so that we might be naked and unashamed before him, fully united with him through faith.

Wrap your mind around this. When God instituted marriage—the joining of two lives into one not only in sexual intimacy but in emotional and relational and spiritual intimacy—the most profound mystery to which this union pointed was the union of Christ and the church. As glorious as human marriage can be, it is but a shadow of the one true marriage.

When I think of the beautiful marriages Rachael and I have observed, I think of sacrifice. We know a husband who took a significant career demotion so he could move his family to a climate where his wife, who has a chronic illness, could thrive physically. We know a couple where both husband and wife sacrificed career aspirations so they could build a ministry life together. An older woman in our church takes care of her ailing husband, whose mental decline has made him meanspirited and unappreciative. I'm sure you can think of stories of sacrifices made for the good of the relationship.

But none of these noble stories matches the good news that "Christ loved the church and gave himself up for her." Jesus' love for his people took him to the cross, where he died for our sins to cleanse us, wash us, purify us, and present us to himself. This is not a sacrifice for an equal partner. This is the holy Son of God taking us in all our spiritual infidelity and paying the highest price to transform us into a bride that shines with the very splendor of our Lover, so that Paul can describe who we are becoming as "without spot or wrinkle or any such thing . . . holy and without blemish" (Eph. 5:27).

The reason the church's intimacy with Christ surpasses any other love is because he transforms our broken, unfaithful hearts to experience this divine union. In case you haven't figured it out, we're the ones who mess up relationships. It's our fickle, self-centered, stunted, deformed hearts that sabotage true love. And in Christ we have a Bridegroom who makes our hearts new.

And one day, Revelation 19:8 tells us, we will "clothe [ourselves] with fine linen, bright and pure," and the church's love for her Christ will be consummated at the marriage of the Lamb. It will be a feast to end all feasts as we celebrate the marriage to end all marriages. And all those longings, all that loneliness, all those hang-ups, all that resistance to God's love will crumble like a feeble dam as the flood of divine love washes everything away and sweeps us into an eternity of knowing and being known, of loving and being loved.

What Are We Waiting For?

Where does this leave us now? For what exactly are we longing today? If the story ends with a wedding feast, what is the current picture?

One particular interaction Jesus had with John the Baptist's disciples locates where we are, and it may not be what you expect. They noted the fact that they and the Pharisees fasted, but Jesus' disciples did not. In response Jesus asked them, "Can the wedding guests mourn as long as the bridegroom is with them? The days will come when the bridegroom is taken away from them, and then they will fast" (Matt. 9:15).

I will never forget the conversation I had with one of my

seminary professors about this text. I assumed it described some ancient Jewish wedding tradition that would make sense of this removal of the bridegroom. But he shared the view most scholars hold—this describes an unexpected, jarring, violent removal of a bridegroom from the middle of the wedding celebration.[26]

Picture the scenario now. You are attending one of those weddings where everyone agrees that this is a match made in heaven. The day is beautiful, the music is perfect, and as the couple repeats their vows, everyone in the room feels excitement that these two are finally together. As the new couple is presented, out of nowhere a black SUV crashes through the chapel door and smoke bombs go off, and when the dust settles, the bridegroom is gone!

Do you feel the shock? The confusion? The disorientation?

Welcome to the disciples' experience of Jesus' ascension. These men had hoped their whole lives for the Messiah. They expected one coming as a conquering king. The cross was so foreign to their concept of what the Messiah would do that Peter rebuked Jesus when he predicted his suffering, rejection, and death. Then, after Jesus' resurrection, the disciples hoped the suffering and the waiting were all finally over, asking Jesus, "Lord, will you at this time restore the kingdom to Israel?" (Acts 1:6). The Bridegroom had risen from the dead and they were ready for the wedding reception and the happily ever after!

Their expectations were upended yet again. Jesus said it was not theirs to know the Father's timeline but to be his Spirit-filled witnesses to the ends of the earth. Then, "as they were looking on, he was lifted up, and a cloud took him out of their sight" (v. 9). The Bridegroom was taken away. Now it is time to fast—to abstain periodically from good things in order to focus our attention on the best thing—the Bridegroom's return.

We will address the "what" and "how" of fasting in chapter 9, but here I want us to feel the "why." We fast because the one who loves us more than he loved his own life has been removed from us. We fast because our fairy-tale ending was violently disrupted and the Hero isn't here anymore. We fast because we want to remember that we are never fully at home until we are with our Bridegroom. We fast because it is our way of experiencing in our bodies what we feel in our hearts—a hunger, a craving, a longing to be with our Christ. We fast because we do not want to cave in to the allurements of this age when our true life belongs in the age to come with Jesus. We fast as those betrothed to one husband who desire to nurture "a sincere and pure devotion to Christ" (2 Cor. 11:2–3).

Giving Voice to the Longing

Let's bring this focus on fasting for our one true Love to the very real experience of loneliness. Loneliness can be a challenging reality to name in our lives, yet recent societal shifts make it pervasive. The deterioration of institutions and fracturing of our political and religious tribes exacerbate our sense of disconnection. Our online lives afford us communication but rarely communion. Add to that a pandemic that required quarantine and distancing, and the equation adds up to increased alienation.

During such times, it can be exponentially challenging to walk through life without that partner who is always there, whether that stems from being in a difficult marriage or living alone. I pray that God will provide you with the companionship you long for through close friendships that are also marked by intimacy, faithfulness, and sacrifice. It is not good for us to be alone, and the lives of Jesus, Paul, and others show us that we can find the relational connection for which we are made outside of marriage.

Understanding that Jesus expects us to fast and watch and wait for his return can remind us that loneliness is a part of our fallen world that will draw to a final end at the coming of our Bridegroom. All of our relationships are imperfect. Even as we seek to build the healthiest connections here with one another, we hunger for that pure, perfect, and never-ending union with Christ that will be realized on the day he returns.

Yet even as we name our loneliness, we hold to the truth that we are not entirely alone. The disciples who saw their Lord taken into heaven and heard the message of his return received the outpouring of the Holy Spirit soon after. Along with empowering their witness to Christ, the Spirit *was* the presence of Christ with them, such that Paul could equate the indwelling of the Holy Spirit with the indwelling of Christ himself (Rom. 8:9–10).

By this Spirit we, the bride of Christ, cry out for the return of the Lover of our souls even as we know his presence by faith. This is the note of expectation on which the New

Testament ends, the sustained chord of pining that awaits its final resolution: "The Spirit and the Bride say, 'Come.' And let the one who hears say, 'Come.' And let the one who is thirsty come; let the one who desires take the water of life without price. . . . He who testifies to these things says, 'Surely I am coming soon.' Amen. Come, Lord Jesus!" (Rev. 22:17, 20).

Questions for Reflection

1. How does your experience of joy and difficulty in your marriage or singleness affect how you think of Jesus as the Bridegroom?
2. What part of the story of God's relationship with Israel resonates with your experience with God the most?
3. Think of times when you have rejected or discounted God's expressions of kindness and loyalty to you in the pages of Scripture or through events in your life. Why do you think you found it difficult to receive his love?
4. How does understanding the jarring removal of the Bridegroom from the wedding feast change how you anticipate Jesus' return?

CHAPTER 6

THE JUDGE

B ehold, the Judge is standing at the door" (James 5:9).
"Christ Jesus, who is to judge the living and the dead"
(2 Tim. 4:1).

What do you think of when you hear these verses about Jesus returning as the Judge? They may evoke nightmares of showing up to class unprepared for the final exam or walking into your workplace wearing no pants. Any context of being judged—going to court or having a performance review—rarely stirs up joyful anticipation. Most of us have a deep-seated fear of exposure that stays with us throughout our lives.

Yet revelations of the truth can cut both ways, depending on whether you have something to hide or desire the truth to be exposed. During the #metoo movement that began in the fall of 2017, headlines of horrific acts of sexual abuse created a sort of judgment day for predators such as Harvey Weinstein and Bill Cosby. Yet to the relief of scores of their victims who carried secret shame, the truth was finally out. When Ravi Zacharias International Ministries conducted a thorough investigation of their late founder, the report unveiled his multiple sinful acts of abuse over many years. Yet it also vindicated the claims of one victim whom Zacharias's organization had painted publicly to be a litigious money-chaser. When the full story was revealed, her assertions to be a victim of his predation were shown to be true.

If we think of judgment as shining a light, unveiling the reality of things, then anticipating the coming of the Judge can be a welcome hope rather than the stuff of nightmares. And indeed, Jesus' return as Judge is all about shining the light.

Up to this point, the portraits of Jesus' return have focused on what he will look like—not his physical features but the spectacle of his return as Warrior King or Bridegroom. But when the New Testament pictures Jesus as Judge, the emphasis is not only on what he will look like but also on what we will look like in his presence.

Paul expresses this with the Greek verb *phaneroō* (think "epi*phan*y"), which means "to reveal, publicly expose, disclose, make known."[27] It is used throughout the New Testament to describe Jesus' return, most often translated "when he appears" (*phanerōthē*). As part of a word group that involves torches and other lights, it also describes Jesus' appearance as John saw it in Revelation: "His face was like the sun shining [*phainei*] in full strength" (Rev. 1:16). As such, this light illuminates everything around it, in the way that opening curtains on a sunny day sheds light on all the dust in the room. The Lord's coming "will bring to light the things now hidden in darkness and will disclose [*phanerōsei*] the purposes of the heart" (1 Cor. 4:5). So one word describes three aspects of the same event: the appearing of Jesus, the physical appearance of Jesus, and our appearing before him, exposed by his brilliance. When Jesus is fully revealed, what we really are will be fully revealed as well.

What will you look like on that day? What will be exposed? How do you feel about what will be seen? Do you want to hide from the prospect of not being able to hide, run away from the inescapable?

If so, this is an invitation to have your life transformed by Jesus' return. It is an invitation not to look away from the inevitability of being revealed but to be shaped by it. When the apostle Paul anticipated the appearing of "the Lord, the righteous judge," he counted himself among those who "loved his appearing" and expected not to be condemned but to be awarded "the crown of righteousness" (2 Tim. 4:8). Rather than debilitating Paul, the coming reality of revelation motivated him.

More than any of the other portraits of Jesus' return that we will ponder, this vision of Jesus as Judge is the most susceptible to being hijacked by our preconceived notions of judgment day or the shame we have internalized from previous experiences of exposure. So we are going to allow Paul's three treatments of judgment to guide us toward his disposition of loving this day of Jesus' appearing. Like a child taking her cues from her parents in a new and potentially frightening situation, we will learn from Paul how pondering this future judgment can positively shape how we live today.

Before You Panic

Let me share two preliminary words of encouragement, especially for those already feeling a degree of panic over this topic.

First, if you are truly in Christ, then judgment is nothing to fear. Before Paul wrote to the Corinthians about what Jesus would judge at his return, he instilled in them a confidence that Jesus himself would "sustain you to the end, guiltless in the day of our Lord Jesus Christ" (1 Cor. 1:8). He did not teach them about coming assessments to cause them to doubt their salvation or to suggest that they had better work harder if they wanted to pass the test. Their hope of salvation lay in Christ from beginning to end. Paul's confidence was not in the Corinthians' effort but in God's power: "God is faithful, by whom you were called into the fellowship of his Son, Jesus Christ our Lord" (1 Cor. 1:9). If you trust in Christ alone to save you, then you have nothing to fear. "There is therefore now no condemnation for those who are in Christ Jesus" (Rom. 8:1).

Second, focusing on Jesus as Judge could actually set you free. If you are anything like me, you already allow yourself, sometimes unconsciously, to live under the judgment of others every day. Whether you are a young mother scrolling through the Instagram feed of picture-perfect moms, a pastor looking at the growing ministry of others, or a homeowner who can't stop noticing how much nicer your neighbors' landscaping is than yours, we all allow ourselves to be judged through constant comparison. Let's be honest, we have nightmares about hearing the ridicule of our peers, not standing before the judgment throne of God.

What if a focus on Jesus' return as Judge could set us free from that? What if dialing up our concern about his assessment would dial down our obsession over the assessment of others? As we launch into Paul's writing on this, let us receive the Judge's coming as a gift that can set us free from others' critiques and motivate us to live in congruence with our trust in him.

Here Comes the Judge

What exactly will Jesus judge?

Throughout his correspondence with the Corinthians, Paul writes about three aspects of our lives that will be exposed at Jesus' coming: our motives, our deeds, and our gospel work. What we will explore was written not in a vacuum but in the context of the Corinthians' intense criticism of Paul and his ministry. We will find that Paul looked to Jesus' return as a refuge, his final word as Judge a true hope of vindication.[28]

Our Motives

Paul was the Corinthians' "father in Christ Jesus through the gospel" (1 Cor. 4:15). The Corinthians, in turn, were like teenagers telling their parents, "You're doing it wrong," questioning numerous aspects of Paul's ministry from his lack of eloquence to his embarrassingly low salary. They compared him to other gospel preachers and formed cliques around which minister they preferred.

Notably, Paul's response is not to reject their scrutiny. Rather, he asserts that any human assessment of his motives—whether the Corinthians' assessment or his own—is inadequate. "But with me it is a very small thing that I should be judged by you or by any human court. In fact, I do not even judge myself. For I am not aware of anything against myself, but I am not thereby acquitted" (1 Cor. 4:3–4).

Not only were the Corinthians immature ("infants in Christ," 1 Cor. 3:1), any judgment they delivered on Paul would be premature. Not all of the evidence is on display; not all of the facts are on the table. Until the day that they are, the Corinthians' proclamations would be insufficient. So Paul points to the judgment that will actually matter: "It is the Lord who judges me. Therefore do not pronounce judgment before the time, before the Lord comes, who will bring to light the things now hidden in darkness and will disclose the purposes of the heart. Then each one will receive his commendation from God" (1 Cor. 4:4–5).

As Paul looked forward to this judgment when the Lord comes, he did so expecting to receive commendation or praise from God. This echoes Peter's encouragement to the suffering believers of Asia that their faith, now being tested through various trials, would "be found to result in praise and glory and honor at the revelation of Jesus Christ" (1 Peter 1:7). Jesus will return not as a harsh professor waiting to pounce on every misplaced comma but as the Judge coming to shine light on the faithfulness of his people.

This should affect how we think of ourselves and others. Regarding ourselves, Paul writes, "I do not even judge myself" (1 Cor. 4:3). Paul is not his own judge; rather, "It is the Lord who judges me" (v. 4). Yet this does not stop Paul from noting, "I am not aware of anything against myself." While he refuses to make a final verdict about himself, Paul does not ignore evidence.

As you read this, you may know something against yourself. There may be "things now hidden in darkness"—images you've been viewing on your smartphone, a second set of books for your business that tell the real story, or threats you have been making to subordinates out of the earshot of others. Or there may be "purposes of the heart" underneath otherwise godly activities—the pride underneath your public prayers, the attention you crave for your generosity, the resentment that drives your decision at a committee meeting. There is no way to soft-pedal this: if you are hiding something now, it will not be hidden when Jesus returns in his brilliance. So expose it now through confession to God and to others whose presence in those hidden places can prepare you for the light of Jesus on that final day.

I write this aware that some are given to obsessive self-examination and fear of God's abandonment as much as others are prone to give themselves a free pass to sin. Wherever you are on that spectrum, make your aim to trust wholly in Christ—resting in his work, not your effort—and allow the Spirit to do his job of identifying sin.

The reality of Jesus' coming as Judge also affects how we think of the judgment of others. Paul's response to the

Corinthians' criticism reminds me of the work our sound guy does at church. On a particular song, he knows that one praise team member will sing the lead while the other three vocalists will sing harmony. So he turns up the volume of the lead singer on the soundboard while he lowers the volume of the others.

Paul wants the Corinthians to know that their criticism of his ministry is "a very small thing." He is going to turn their volume down to a two while he keeps Jesus' volume up to a full ten (unless the speaker goes to eleven). His simple statement "It is the Lord who judges me" simultaneously frees him from the assessment of those who do not know his motives or see the big picture and keeps him focused on the one who does.

Yet notice that Paul calls their criticism "a very small thing," not "nothing." He turns their volume down to two, not zero. To the degree that their assessment is in harmony with the lead vocalist, Jesus, Paul can receive their criticism as applicable and actionable. To the degree that their assessment is out of tune with what Paul knows to be the heart of Christ and his calling to gospel ministry, Paul can listen primarily to his Master's input.

A life tuned in to the great voice of Jesus sets us free from a life made small by the expectations and disappointments of others. I have lost count of the number of times I have leaned on Paul's assessment of the Corinthians' criticism as "a very small thing" when facing criticism myself. It empowers me to listen to the critic while not feeling my world turn upside down. This allows me to pay attention to what I need to take from their words rather than licking my wounds. If the experience of being criticized does upend me emotionally, this unveils how small the return of Christ has become to me and exposes my need to refocus my anticipation on Jesus' return as Judge.

Our Deeds

In 2 Corinthians Paul says there is something else that will be exposed when "we must all appear before the judgment seat of Christ." Each one will "receive what is due for what he has done in the body, whether good or evil" (2 Cor. 5:10).

Similar to 1 Corinthians 4, this look to the day of Christ's judgment is set in the context of the Corinthians' judgment of Paul's ministry, specifically spurred on by outside voices that sought to delegitimize Paul. Again Paul redirects the gaze of his spiritual children upward to the one true Judge. By centering his legitimacy on the assessment of Jesus, not his own or theirs, Paul can honestly say that "we are not commending ourselves to you again but giving you cause to boast about us, so that you may be able to answer those who boast about outward appearance and not about what is in the heart" (2 Cor. 5:12).

If you have ever had someone size you up, critique superficial traits, or make unwarranted assessments, hopefully you can appreciate why Paul found his center of gravity and ultimate motivation in the thought of standing before the judgment seat of Christ.

The English translation of "we must all appear before the judgment seat of Christ" obscures the stunning way in which

Paul articulates this. He uses the *phaneroō* verb not to describe *what* will be revealed but *who* will be revealed. The verse could be better translated, "We must all *be revealed* before the judgment seat of Christ." Lest we ever distance ourselves from our motives or deeds, Paul reminds us that what will be revealed before Jesus at his return is us. As Ralph Martin puts it, each of us must "appear" before Christ the Judge— "not in the sense of a simple 'showing up' but in the sense of being laid bare, for all the world to see the true nature of one's character."[29]

Again, this was a welcome prospect for Paul as he faced the present judgments of "those who boast about outward appearance and not about what is in the heart." The point is not that God will judge each individual motive, thought, conversation, and action. Paul's language about the judgment of what one "has done in the body" is not whether each discrete moment is "good or evil" (v. 10) but whether the overall character it reveals is good or evil.

Think of this in terms of how we evaluate college students on their work. I studied music in college, and for three hours a day I practiced piano, working my way through this Brahms sonata and that Bach fugue. But regardless of how my piano pieces sounded in the practice room throughout the semester, there was only one performance that counted for the grade: juries. If the word juries strikes fear in your heart, you understand the weight they carry for music students. The name of my major was Piano Performance, so the jury of piano professors assessed one thing: Could I perform? It was a high-pressure moment of judgment.

However, I also had friends who studied English composition, art, and architecture. In these majors, there was typically no big test at the end of the semester, no single performance that strongly determined how their mastery of the material was judged. Rather it was one writing assignment, one painting, one skyscraper model at a time. And at the end of the semester, the cumulative work was assessed. While there was a big push to finish the last assignment at the end, there weren't too many surprises on the grade, since the work had been accumulating for months.

This second model is the kind of judgment Paul describes in these three texts. Jesus will not administer some test or ask you a question to see whether you pass or fail. There is no required performance. He will simply shed light on your entire life to see what is revealed about the work that you did day in and day out. So you could say that judgment day is happening right now as you read this and as you go on to the next thing. For Paul it was happening as he dealt with the Corinthians. And this prospect of light being shed on his labor did not terrify him. Paul could, in the context of the judgment, speak of his confidence before God and affirm that "what we are is known to God" (2 Cor. 5:8, 11). He knows this because "we walk by faith, not by sight" (v. 7). His fundamental relationship with Jesus was one of trust. By faith he knew Christ and was known by Christ, so he anticipated standing before the judgment seat with assurance that he would belong to Christ forever.

What kind of difference should this make in how we live today? If we are not supposed to freak out at the reality of judgment, if the judgment seat of Christ can be a relief to us amid the indictments of our peers, how are we supposed to live toward the day we will be revealed before Christ?

In the immediate context, Paul shares his two motivators: a desire to please the Lord and the fear of the Lord.

What Motivates Our Deeds? A Desire to Please the Lord.

The prospect of being revealed before the judgment seat of Christ is the reason Paul says in 2 Corinthians 5:9 that "we make it our aim to please him." And the context gives us clues that this is not a fearful supplicant hoping to please someone with power, lest he get punished, but an adoring follower who wants nothing more than to please the one who loved him. In writing about being in the body versus being in the Lord's presence, Paul makes it clear that "we would rather be away from the body and at home with the Lord" (v. 8). His singular desire in life was to know Christ, and thus he yearned to be in the presence of Christ. But wherever he was, he wanted his life to please Jesus Christ.

You have probably experienced this dynamic at a human level. My grandmother was one of the most important people in my life. Beyond usual family gatherings, she hosted my brother and me for a week every summer, spoiling us with gifts and outings, most notably an epic trip to Showbiz Pizza. She fed us with the best Southern cooking in Savannah, taught us life lessons in everyday moments, and gave us an emotional safety net of knowing we were loved regardless of our success in sports or academics.

So when I stood next to Mimi's coffin at the funeral home on the eve of preaching her funeral, I looked at her lifeless body and said, "I want to get it right tomorrow." I stayed up until 2:00 in the morning writing her funeral message because I wanted to please this woman who had given so much to me. She had delighted in me every day of my life, and I wanted to make her proud in return.

This is the posture Paul had toward Jesus, the one "who loved me and gave himself for me" (Gal. 2:20). Paul remained astonished by Jesus' mercy throughout his days and simply wanted to please the Lord. No hustling for approval, only pure gratitude and love. This drove Paul's preaching of the gospel to those who had not heard about Jesus, his patient training of new believers in how to follow Jesus, his confrontation of sin and conflict and false teaching among Jesus' people, and his investment in next-generation leaders.

What Motivates Our Deeds? The Fear of the Lord. Just as the coming judgment grounds Paul's desire to please the Lord, it also informs his fear of the Lord. "Therefore," he writes after noting that our deeds will be judged, "knowing the fear of the Lord, we persuade others" (2 Cor. 5:11). Paul knew his life of faith in Christ would render a verdict of "good" before the judgment seat of Christ, but he did not know about others. So his proclamation of Christ and the reconciliation with God that Christ offers was driven by his reverence for the coming judgment on all people.

This is complementary, not contradictory, to Paul's desire to please the Lord. Fear without the desire to please leads to servile dread. The desire to please without fear leads to overfamiliarity, the assumption that the divine Son of God's commands are optional. As much as my story about my grandmother is a good analogy, it isn't a perfect one. Jesus isn't my grandmother. Yes, he is the Lover of my soul. But he is also the Judge of the universe. This demands awe. The natural responses to being in a relationship with Jesus Christ are both a desire to please him and a healthy fear of him. This reverence can fuel urgent and heartfelt pleas with our neighbors to believe the gospel. Against strong cultural currents that validate all religious beliefs and reject claims of exclusivity, our focus on Jesus' final judgment keeps the call to repentance and trust in Christ on the tips of our tongues.

Our Gospel Work

The third thing that will be exposed at Jesus' coming is our gospel work.

The Corinthians' criticism of Paul's ministry flowed from values rooted in Corinth rather than Christ. Theirs was a culture of power and wealth. The rock stars of the day were traveling orators who could pack amphitheaters with their recitations of Homer's *Odyssey* or impromptu speeches. By Corinthian standards, someone like Paul who did not charge for his ministry and did not deliver his sermons with professional eloquence was tragically unimpressive. And they let him know about it.

Paul's response to this was not only to remind them that Jesus was his Judge, not them, but also to warn them about the consequences of this very Corinthian orientation regarding their own ministry work. Using the language of constructing a building, where he is the general contractor and the Corinthians who continued his work are subcontractors, Paul expected that "each one's work will become manifest [*phaneron*], for the Day will disclose it, because it will be revealed by fire, and the fire will test what sort of work each one has done" (1 Cor. 3:13). The work will be revealed on the day of the Lord because, as the previous verse states, some of the building materials are flammable ("wood, hay, straw") while others are not ("gold, silver, precious stones"), thus contrasting work that will endure with that which will not.[30]

As Paul looks to the Day, the revealing of Jesus Christ, he knows that work done in people's lives that was not built with the gospel will be burned up. Those who placed their faith in philosophical fads or popular preachers—but not in the gospel—will not endure the fire of judgment. Paul has already laid the foundation, Jesus Christ (1 Cor. 3:11), and the only work that will last is that which is also grounded in this gospel: "Jesus Christ and him crucified" (1 Cor. 2:2). So the prospect of Jesus' coming motivates Paul to build with the good news about Jesus. He motivated the Corinthians to do the same. Toward the end of this letter, he begins chapter 15 by reminding them of the gospel—the durable news of Christ's death and resurrection—and closes the chapter with the encouragement, based on the sure return of Christ, to "be steadfast, immovable, always abounding in the work of the Lord, knowing that in the Lord your labor is not in vain" (1 Cor. 15:58).

This brings a laser focus to our ministry: Am I pointing

others to trust in Jesus Christ alone? We will explore the ministry that anticipating Jesus produces more thoroughly in chapter 12. Suffice it to say that what will endure the building inspection are not the trendy pop-culture references, the sweet guitar solos, or the viral social-media posts. Christ will endure, as will the lives and works built on him.

The Simple Look to Jesus

We opened this chapter observing how powerful men have covered their deeds in darkness through legal action and the sheer force of their celebrity. In my years as a pastor, I have heard parallel stories in their local, unreported forms time and time again. Whether these survivors were curled up in the fetal position, weeping, or blank and detached, they told me about pastors with kinglike authority, parents dismissive of their children's claims, and perpetrators who leveraged their credibility to persuade the community of their innocence. These covered their deeds or the deeds of others in darkness, isolating the abused to carry his or her shame alone.

Perhaps you have been cast into darkness through similar means. False rumors about your intentions or integrity have gained traction in your organization. Assumptions based on your manner or appearance have overwhelmed the reality of who you are. Perhaps you are a police officer or a priest faithfully doing your work before God during a time when public stories about your colleagues make others immediately suspicious of you. Perhaps the most recent conspiracy theory on social media has led your family members or longtime friends to make puzzling assertions about you. You feel powerless to set the record straight, to convince others of who you really are and why you do what you do.

There is a simple way of life open to us when we anticipate Jesus' appearing as Judge. The light he will shine on that day will illuminate the true state of everything—our motives, our deeds, and our gospel work. This bright hope relativizes the criticism of others and centers our definition of success and life well lived around the one who gave his life for us. Whether or not our pursuit of faithfulness to Jesus is visible to others in this age, it will be manifest in the age to come. So we labor in hope, knowing that our labor is not in vain.

We can do this knowing that we stand in a noble line of the misrepresented. Jesus knew his own reputation: "Look at him! A glutton and a drunkard, a friend of tax collectors and sinners!" (Matt. 11:19). Paul endured untold slander, being considered by many "the scum of the world, the refuse of all things" (1 Cor. 4:13). Yet Jesus also taught that "wisdom is justified by her deeds" (Matt. 11:19), and Paul walked in his calling with confidence, knowing that the assessment of Jesus would be all that mattered. In a world where social media amplifies the opinions of anyone with a mobile device and where charitable discourse is on the decline, let us turn down the volume of the critics and turn up the voice of our Lord as we walk in obedience to him and anticipate hearing, "Well done, good and faithful servant" (Matt. 25:23).

Questions for Reflection

1. What initial reaction does the thought of Jesus' return as Judge bring up for you? Why do you think that is?

2. Are you facing unwarranted criticism? How could fixing your hope on Jesus' return as Judge change how you handle that criticism? How might it free you from comparing yourself with others?

3. What would it look like for you to be motivated both by a desire to please the Lord and by the fear of the Lord—both flowing out of a life of trust in Jesus?

4. As you think of the "building" work God has called you to, are you building with the gospel, pointing the people to whom you minister to Jesus Christ and him crucified? If not, what would it look like for you to start doing so?

CHAPTER 7

THE RESURRECTING ONE

Often when we read the Bible, we have to translate the terms and times into our own context. What does justification mean? Where is the Jordan River? How exactly does one gird up his loins?

Then there are times when the ancient word needs no translation. Such is the case with Paul's description of life in the body. Using the metaphor of a tent, Paul writes, "In this tent we groan" (2 Cor. 5:2). Perhaps you feel that right now. Whether you have muscular pain, chronic fatigue, or depression, you groan out of your physical discomfort. Even if you feel fine at the moment, a quick scan of family, friends, and neighbors gives voice to the groans of those with coronary heart disease, diabetes, cancer, anxiety, arthritis, and post-traumatic stress disorder. Add on to that the layers of relational and societal pain—betrayal, prejudice, abuse, war, famine—and it is almost too much to bear. In these bodies, these tents, we groan.

Jesus is hope to those who feel ruin in this life. And we

can hope fully in his return because he comes as one who has been resurrected from the dead.

If you grew up in the church, the phrase "from the dead"—used more than fifty times in the New Testament—might be so familiar to you that you haven't paused to hear it. "The dead" implies those who have succumbed to the ruin, whose groaning has given way to the death rattle, whose bodies now lie in tombs and caskets and urns. Jesus, God the Son made flesh, joined them. He was crucified and buried. He was among the dead.

This is crucial to remember as we engage the hope of resurrection. Often our experience of physical decline leaves us emotionally disinclined toward hoping in much of anything. My family walked through a long season of physical exhaustion and emotional depression because of hidden mold exposure in our house. In those low seasons when we felt like we were drowning, a chipper messenger saying, "Just hope in resurrection!" would have felt out of touch. But what does not feel out of touch is the news that Jesus willingly entered the deterioration we felt in our weariness and frayed emotions, that he went beyond our level of illness all the way down to that place among the dead.

So if you feel your mortality acutely as you read this, I pray you will feel Jesus' solidarity with your downward trajectory even as we focus on the hope of Jesus' upward trajectory of new, eternal life.

Because Jesus did not remain among the dead. He took a round-trip journey up a one-way street. He defeated death.

His shout of victory replaced the groan of agony. He was sown a perishable body and was raised imperishable. He was sown in dishonor and raised in glory (1 Cor. 15:42–43). As he, risen and glorified, said to John in Revelation 1:17–18, "I am the first and the last, and the living one. I died, and behold I am alive forevermore, and I have the keys of Death and Hades."

Jesus is hope to those who groan because his resurrection is the first of many. Paul calls him "the firstfruits of those who have fallen asleep" then spells out the timeline of resurrection: "Christ the firstfruits, then at his coming those who belong to Christ" (1 Cor. 15:20, 23). Just as the first apple from the tree assures the farmer that there are more bushels to come from the orchard, the single resurrected body of Jesus of Nazareth assures those who belong to Christ that they will share the same destiny.

As glorious as this news is, our focus in this chapter goes beyond the mere completion of what Jesus set in motion with his resurrection. We will look at what Jesus will do when he returns. For he will come not only as the resurrect*ed* one but as the resurrect*ing* one. In his resurrection Jesus was not only a living being like the first Adam but, as the last Adam, "a life-giving spirit" (1 Cor. 15:45). Jesus will return to change you, to make you forever new.

Speaking Life

My wife and I have made unique forays into cultivating life in our home. Like many, we have had pet dogs that, despite my curmudgeonly disposition toward them, have brought joy and humor to our family. Unlike most people, we turned our large back yard into an urban farm when we lived in Phoenix, raising chickens and keeping goats. For about four years my wife milked three goats every morning. Our children helped with filling the goats' water, replenishing the feeding trough, and cleaning out their pen. The chickens, then, were happy to dig through the compost pile for worms, and we were happy to retrieve their eggs and cook the bright orange yolks that only farm eggs produce.

But as much as we thrived in cultivating animal life, the one thing we have yet to master is plant life. We planted trees in the back yard, and the goats broke through the fencing to eat the bark and knock them down. We planted trees in the front yard, and despite all our watering efforts, they shriveled up and died under the fierce Arizona sun. All the flowers we have planted have made it through only one season, if that. We were even given a succulent at a white elephant party that did not survive. When I saw this sturdy plant turn brown, the words of comedian Demetri Martin came to mind: "I am less nurturing than a desert!" Whatever the opposite of a green thumb is, that's what we have. It's like everything we touch in the plant world dies.

At his return, Jesus will be the opposite. Everything he touches will live. To be more accurate, everything to which he speaks will come to life.

We see a preview of this in the Gospels. When Jesus was on earth, he spoke to the dead little girl, "'Talitha cumi,' which means, 'Little girl, I say to you, arise.' And immediately the girl got up and began walking" (Mark 5:41–42). Likewise, after Lazarus was dead for days, Jesus had the stone rolled away from the tomb, stood at the mouth of the death cave, and "cried out with a loud voice, 'Lazarus, come out.' The man who had died came out" (John 11:43–44).

But on that final day Jesus will do more than resuscitate a recently deceased person. As Jesus himself taught, "An hour is coming, and is now here, when the dead will hear the voice of the Son of God, and those who hear will live" (John 5:25).

This will not simply bring new life into old bones but will be an entire transformation. As Paul wrote, "Our citizenship is in heaven, and from it we await a Savior, the Lord Jesus Christ, who will transform our lowly body to be like his glorious body, by the power that enables him even to subject all things to himself" (Phil. 3:20–21). Out of the bones and ashes of your dead body, Jesus, the life-giving spirit, will bring about an entirely new body—what Paul calls elsewhere an imperishable, glorious, spiritual body (1 Cor. 15:42–44). He will return as the Resurrecting One. As he promised four times in John's gospel about each one who trusts in him, "I will raise him up on the last day" (John 6:40; see also vv. 39, 44, and 54).

The Resurrection Body

Have you tried to imagine this moment? What will it be like to inhabit a transformed, resurrected body? This is one of those mental exercises that hurts your brain because you have to imagine so many aspects of your physical life being so radically different.

Yet the effort is worth it. If the hope of the resurrection that Jesus will bring about at his return is to carry us through the deterioration of this life, we need to set our hopes as high as the New Testament does.

This exercise reminds me of a card game our family enjoys called Set. Players look at the same group of cards with objects on them and process four features on each card—the number of objects, their color, filling, and shape. To make a set, you have to find three cards where the features are all the same or all different; for example, one card has one purple-striped diamond, a second card has two red-striped ovals, and the third card has three green-striped squiggles. That's a set. It is a delightful game, but it stretches the brain. Part of the entertainment is hearing the grunts and groans of players who are trying to hold all these categories in their heads at the same time as they calculate whether three cards make a set.

The New Testament identifies at least four ways in which our new bodies will be greater than our current bodies. Holding them all in mind at the same time may stretch your brain. But it is worth the work to know our robust resurrection hope. Let's walk through them one at a time, then pull together the composite of the resurrection body.

Permanent, Not Temporary

After calling our bodies tents, Paul writes that what we long for is a house: "a building from God, a house not made with hands, eternal in the heavens" (2 Cor. 5:1). Just as the sturdiest camping tents eventually fade, tear, fray, and leak, our bodies over time cramp, sag, tire, and, well, leak. Because of the fall, they no longer last. Jesus comes to create something more akin to brick than canvas, a physical home that will endure, world without end.

Imperishable, Not Perishable

For those of us over a certain age, it is nearly impossible to imagine living in a body that is impervious to deterioration, but that is exactly what Paul promises at the return of Christ. "This perishable body must put on the imperishable, and this mortal body must put on immortality." This is synonymous with his statement that "death is swallowed up in victory" (1 Cor. 15:53–54). Death is the inevitable destination of mortality. The victory of Christ over death translates into an eternity of living in imperishable bodies with God and his people. Nothing about our bodies will die—no mental decline, no seizing up of the back, no loss of bodily functions. We will not utter the words "I can't _____ like I used to" about any activity. Never again to be distracted by pain or disease, we will enjoy God and his people in the new creation forever.

Glorious, Not Lowly

Paul uses degrees of glory in nature to communicate the qualitative difference between our bodies now and the resurrection body to come: "There is one glory of the sun, and another glory of the moon" (1 Cor. 15:41). Scientists can now put a number on what every observer of heavenly bodies throughout the centuries has known: the sun appears 400,000 times brighter than a full moon.

This is in the ballpark of how much more glorious our new bodies will be than our current ones. In chapter 3 we saw the frighteningly, blindingly brilliant state of Jesus in his resurrection body. Such will be our existence. When Jesus will "transform our lowly body to be like his glorious body" (Phil. 3:21), this will not be a mere improvement to the most attractive, fit, or healthy human body possible. This is an upgrade to a transcendent level of existence. This is not replacing your tricycle with a nicer tricycle but replacing your tricycle with a Lamborghini.

Let us not mince words: You will be glorious.

Does that make you uncomfortable to think about? It does for me. After all, we are to keep our focus on Christ, not ourselves, right? But perhaps our Christ-centeredness should rather release us to hope fully in what Christ will change us into at his return. Our true identity is now "hidden with Christ in God," but "when Christ who is your life appears, then you also will appear with him in glory" (Col. 3:3–4). "Just as we have borne the image of the man of dust, we shall also bear the image of the man of heaven" (1 Cor. 15:49). On that day you will be glorious. Because of the Resurrecting One, you will shine with a brilliance that, were you to see it now, would blind you!

Spiritual, Not Natural

At first blush, the distinction between spiritual and natural sounds like our resurrection bodies will be ghostlike rather than tangible. This is the opposite of what Paul meant by the terms (which admittedly are difficult to translate into English) and certainly the opposite of what Jesus' resurrection body was like. While he vanished from the Emmaus road disciples and appeared in a locked room following his resurrection, he set the record straight with his disciples, who "thought they saw a spirit." Jesus said, "See my hands and my feet, that it is I myself. Touch me, and see. For a spirit does not have flesh and bones as you see that I have" (Luke 24:37, 39). He then asked for something to eat and ate some fish in front of them.

If this was true of the resurrection prototype, Jesus, what does it mean that we will have a spiritual body rather than a natural one? As it turns out, the distinction is about the home for which the body is fashioned. "The first man was from the earth, a man of dust; the second man is from heaven" (1 Cor. 15:47). David Garland explains it this way: "In the same way that those in Adam bear Adam's characteristics in their home on earth, those in Christ will be made like Christ, with spiritual bodies appropriate for their new heavenly existence."[31]

I write this only a week after taking my twin teenaged sons to one of the largest amusement parks in our state. We rode on a rollercoaster that answered the question, "How can you experience a three-hundred-foot drop straight down without dying?" The answer is to be fully buckled down to the car with seatbelts and over-the-shoulder restraints. My son's glasses didn't survive the drop; thankfully we did. Those restraints enabled us to do something otherwise impossible.

Our spiritual bodies will enable us to do something that God had previously told Moses was impossible: "You cannot see my face, for man shall not see me and live" (Ex. 33:20). Yet in these new bodies, crafted for dwelling with the divine, we will not be blinded by the brilliant splendor of Jesus' uncreated glory. We will not fall as though dead every time we hear his roaring voice. Our bodies will be fit to engage the joys of heaven—indescribable now, spiritually native then.

Putting It All Together

Are you ready to put all of these together? At his coming, Jesus will transform your deteriorating or decaying body into a permanent, imperishable, glorious, spiritual body. As you walk down streets of gold and swim in the river by the tree of life, you will never pull a hamstring or diminish in energy from one century to the next. Shining with the brilliance of the sun, your body will image forth the glory of God as fully as your character will. And while you will never cease feeling wonder in the presence of the Almighty, neither will you have to squint in his presence. Moses will no longer hide in the rock to see the Shekinah glory. Isaiah will never again say "woe is me" in the presence of the King. John will not fall as dead before the divine splendor. We will have hearts and bodies fit for this eternal experience of God.

To take this a step farther, join me in feeling the wonder that Jesus, the Resurrecting One, will transform you into this glorious body "in a moment, in the twinkling of an eye, at the last trumpet. For the trumpet will sound, and the dead will be raised imperishable, and we shall be changed" (1 Cor. 15:52).

This is what we see when we hope fully in Jesus' return as the resurrected Resurrecting One: that instantaneous transformation into a body like his. I would say that it is like something out of a fairy tale or a superhero movie, but no special effects could do this moment justice. It will be the event of your lifetime.

The Whole Creation Groans

As we anticipate that moment, our groaning in these tents echoes the groans of the whole creation that awaits not only our resurrection but its own release from decay. Since God's pronouncements of judgment at the fall, the deterioration of the creation has been inextricably bound with our moral, spiritual, and physical ruin. As Paul writes in Romans 8:20–21, "The creation was subjected to futility, not willingly, but because of him who subjected it, in hope that the creation itself will be set free from its bondage to corruption and obtain the freedom of the glory of the children of God." As brutal as your back spasms may be, the convulsions of this planet in earthquakes and drought, thorns and thistles, cry out for resurrection.

Paul sets this level of groaning at one of the highest known to woman: "the pains of childbirth" (v. 22). Paul draws here on a common metaphor used in the day—the "birth pains of the Messiah" that the Jewish community believed would take place before the Messiah came to consummate God's kingdom. Jesus himself used this reference when he spoke of the earth's wars and natural disasters as "the beginning of the birth pains" (Mark 13:8).

What hopeful Jews of Jesus' day didn't expect—whether or not they believed him to be the Messiah—was that the Messiah would bear these agonizing birth pangs and bring about the beginning of the new creation in his own body. In John 16, Jesus, looking to his near crucifixion, told his disciples, "When a woman is giving birth, she has sorrow because her hour has come, but when she has delivered the baby, she no longer remembers the anguish, for joy that a human being has been born into the world" (John 16:21). He commandeered the familiar Jewish word picture to refer to his impending death and resurrection.

Jesus' intensely personal engagement with the ruin of our world grounds our hope in his future resurrecting work. He bore the physical, emotional, relational, and spiritual anguish of this broken world in his body on the cross. This means that you can come to him as "a man of sorrows and acquainted with grief" (Isa. 53:3), one who knows your pain intimately. And his victorious defeat of death in his own resurrection means that the permanent, imperishable, glorious, spiritual body you await is not wishful thinking but is as real of a hope as the resurrected Jesus who ate fish and appeared to five hundred believers (1 Cor. 15:6).

The death and resurrection of Jesus both portrayed and made possible the destruction and renewal of the cosmos. As we saw in chapter 2, the day of the Lord was on full display at Calvary. So when we look toward Jesus' return, we antic-ipate the death and resurrection of all things—our bodies, this physical creation—made possible by Jesus, "the firstborn of the dead" (Rev. 1:5). In our groaning, we wait expectantly for the day when God's work of making all things new will be consummated.

"But the day of the Lord will come like a thief, and then the heavens will pass away with a roar, and the heavenly bodies will be burned up and dissolved, and the earth and the works that are done on it will be exposed. Since all these things are thus to be dissolved, what sort of people ought you to be in lives of holiness and godliness, waiting for and hastening the coming of the day of God, because of which the heavens will be set on fire and dissolved, and the heavenly bodies will melt as they burn! But according to his promise we are waiting for new heavens and a new earth in which righteousness dwells" (2 Peter 3:10–13).

Until then, we live in a culture that does not share our hope in resurrection. Curiosity about eternal life surfaces in science-fiction shows about uploading our consciousness to the cloud, but the idea that our bodies will be resurrected following the prototype of Jesus is not fixed in our public assumptions. So we leverage all of our scientific knowledge to preserve youth and extend life as long as possible. There is plenty to be said for taking care of our bodies, and we should be grateful for medical procedures that address issues which, in former generations, would have been a death sentence. But counter to our culture, we have to remember that we're camping; we're not at home. These are tents, not castles. We hope in Jesus' return as the Resurrecting One who will make our bodies eternally new.

I think of all the diseases members of my family live with, like celiac and Crohn's and Alzheimer's. I think of church members with cancer, heart disease, bipolar disorder, and undiagnosable chronic illnesses. I think of those spending their days in a nursing home when they thought they would be traveling. Paul's words prove to be so true: "In this tent we groan" (2 Cor. 5:2).

As you groan in your earthly tent and minister to others who feel ruin in their bones, may the Spirit grant you a robust, sturdy hope in Jesus' return to make all things new. May the pain draw you closer to Jesus in gratitude for his promise of renewal. May you sense his nearness to you as one who felt the brokenness of this world in his own body. And may you find deeper community with those who share your experience of bodily pain and who share your hope in the coming of the Resurrecting One.

Questions for Reflection

1. What physical groaning do you feel right now, whether in your body or in the hurts of those in your closest circles?
2. How does Jesus' personal engagement with the deterioration of our world—through his joining the dead and rising again—speak to your situation?

3. If you are one with Jesus by faith, you will receive a resurrection body like his: permanent, imperishable, glorious, and spiritual. Take a couple of minutes to write out what it will be like to live in such a body.

4. What groaning of the whole creation are you observing right now (for example, earthquakes, forest fires, disease, drought)? How might these propel you to greater hope in Jesus' return?

PART 3
RHYTHMS OF ANTICIPATION

Originally when I outlined this book, I launched directly from the portraits of Jesus' appearing into how believing these truths should transform us into pure, passionate followers of Jesus who endure the trials and temptations of this age. But I hit a point where I realized that things weren't clicking for me. There was a disconnect.

I wonder if you have felt a similar disconnect between knowing about Jesus' glorious appearing—even believing it is true—and actual life transformation. I am convinced theoretically about the reality of Jesus' appearing, but I realized that it didn't really change me in noticeable ways. Life gets so busy that it's easy to forget that Jesus is coming again.

So I started looking to God's Word to ask a specific question: What rhythms, habits, or disciplines are offered to help us nurture anticipation for Jesus' appearing? What steps to maintain a posture of hope does the Bible offer? And after scouring God's Word and talking with others who know it well, I found three rhythms of anticipation: gather, fast, and rest. If you think of our journey from here to Jesus' return as a road trip, these are like both guardrails to keep us on the road and road signs to point us ahead.

None of the following chapters are meant to be a comprehensive treatment of church life, fasting, or Sabbath. My primary concern is how each discipline can consistently keep the reality of Jesus' return in front of us and enhance our expectancy to see Christ again. As I have practiced them, I have found my hope mounting over time as my calendar has been shaped by Jesus' return. May this bright hope give you increasing strength as you incorporate these practices into your week.

CHAPTER 8

GATHER

As more people experience their church services online because of the coronavirus pandemic, the question of why Christians gather in the first place has been challenged. Many aspects of church life that once felt indispensable have yet to return postquarantine. For those who are immunocompromised or homebound, the virtual option is a welcome blessing. Yet many for whom health concerns are not a factor now wonder why they would leave the house—much less change out of their pajamas!—when they can turn on the service right there at home.

The pandemic is but one factor in the shakeup the American church faces. Congregations have fractured in response to political and social movements. Individual believers wonder whether they're really at home in churches that have taken one stand or another. With the broadcasting power of social media, many have vocalized their doubts about a variety of church teachings and practices. Church life is in a state of radical change. These dynamics have caused us all to ask, "Why should I go to church?"

One of the verses preachers often use to emphasize the importance of gathering is Hebrews 10:25, which tells us not to neglect meeting together, as is the habit of some. Apparently, people have been skipping church for a few thousand years! But if you read the context of this verse, that phrase isn't just a shaming stick to hit people with but part of a positive vision of church life that looks explicitly to Jesus' return. "And let us consider how to stir up one another to love and good works, not neglecting to meet together, as is the habit of some, but encouraging one another, and all the more as you see the Day drawing near" (vv. 24–25).

What many might read as a mere flourish at the end—"as you see the Day drawing near"—actually carries a tremendous load. The very act of meeting together has an end-times focus. The "one another" work we do is consequential because the Day is consequential, because Jesus' return matters. Following this phrase, the author of Hebrews launches into one of the letter's warning passages that speaks of "a fearful expectation of judgment" (v. 27) for those who become adversaries of Christ.

This necessarily wades into questions of how we understand these warning passages and what exactly they are warning could happen. It is not my intention to adjudicate these thorny and nuanced topics here. Whatever your view of these issues may be, we should be able to agree on two things: we must hold fast to Christ to the end (Heb. 3:14; 1 Cor. 15:2), and we need each other's help to do this.

Gathering, therefore, is not merely something for serious or advanced Christians. It is not a box to be checked off our evangelical to-do list. It is essential to our survival. We need each other. And in this chapter we will look at four ways our gathering nurtures a love for Jesus' appearing.

Before we do, let me acknowledge a few things. I know many people who have long and joyful histories with healthy churches. And I know many who have experienced abuse or neglect in the church, whether by church members or leaders. If you are in the second category, my intent here is not to exacerbate your wounds. I pray that what follows can give you hope in what a healthy church family can be, even if you are still in pursuit of such a community.

For those who are established in a church, let me speak honestly as a pastor. One of the frustrations many pastors face is when church members say, "I've been listening to Pastor _____, who has been emphasizing _____. We never talk about that and could use more of that around here." You can do the math and appreciate the fact that a pastor cannot emphasize everything all the time, and the last thing I want to do is to send you to your pastor with a "you're doing it wrong" memo.

That is why this chapter is aimed at church members. While I hope leaders read and apply this material to the way they "do church," the real change happens from the grass-roots. The emphasis of this chapter is for you as a member of Christ's body to look at how you can bring a new intentionality to your experience of the normal functioning of the church. As you increase in hope, my prayer is that you will become a change agent to inspire others to greater anticipation of Jesus' return.

Hearing God's Promises

One crucial way our gathering with God's people nurtures a robust hope is the solidarity it builds in our hearing God's promises.

The call in Hebrews 10:25 to encourage one another "as you see the Day drawing near" echoes the call in Hebrews 3:13 to "exhort one another every day, as long as it is called 'today,' that none of you may be hardened by the deceitfulness of sin."[32] The cautionary tale that serves as a backdrop to this warning is the Israelites' rebellion in the wilderness. Fresh out of slavery in Egypt, with ten plagues and a parted Red Sea in their recent past, the Israelites following Moses through the desert refused to take the promised land when spies reported that they had seen fortified cities and giants in the land.

The problem, according to Hebrews 4:2, was that even though the wandering Israelites heard the good news of a promised new home, "the message they heard did not benefit them, because they were not united by faith with those who listened."

"United with those who listened"? What exactly does that mean?

Let's recall briefly the context of this wilderness rebellion. Of the twelve spies sent to do reconnaissance in Canaan, ten of them flatly said, "We are not able to go up against the people, for they are stronger than we are" (Num. 13:31). They regaled the people with stories of milk and honey, of large fruit and fertile land. But the story changed quickly when they reported that they also saw high walls and tall men in whose presence the Israelites seemed like grasshoppers. In their minds the whole venture was a nonstarter.

Joshua and Caleb, on the other hand, emphasized not what they saw but what they had heard—the promise of Yahweh to give them the land. This was the promise God spoke to Abraham, Isaac, and Jacob. It was the promise God reiterated to Moses at the burning bush: "I promise that I will bring you up out of the affliction of Egypt to the land of the Canaanites" (Ex. 3:17). Every Israelite at the doorstep of Canaan had heard these promises. But they weren't listening. They chose to allow what had been seen—walls and giants—to overrule what had been heard—God's promise to give them the land.

What they needed was to be "united by faith with those who listened." They needed to be joined with Caleb's trust that "if the LORD delights in us, he will bring us into this land and give it to us, a land that flows with milk and honey. . . . The LORD is with us; do not fear them" (Num. 14:8–9). They needed solidarity with those who walked by faith, not by sight.

And such is our need each day of our journey to the better and abiding country. We need to be united with those who listen to the promises of God. As the author of Hebrews quotes over and over from Psalm 95:7–8, "Today, if you hear his voice, do not harden your hearts as in the rebellion" (Heb. 3:7–8, 15; 4:7).

When you gather with God's people, you gather to hear the promises of God that you will hear in few other places.

119

Advertisers spend billions of dollars inviting you to walk by sight in the new car that will mark your wealth and sophistication, or the beer that, if held just right, will make you breezy and winsome in social interactions. Cable news channels set before you the stories that will ignite the most outrage and, once you've found the right channel for you, reinforce your political assumptions. Software developers have consulted psychologists to maximize the time they can keep you on their apps. By the time you enter the congregation of the redeemed each weekend, your eyes have been bombarded with a cornucopia of promises of immediate delight.

But when we gather together, we gather not for seeing but for hearing, to bolster "the assurance of things hoped for, the conviction of things not seen" (Heb. 11:1). We gather to remember that Jesus is the Warrior King who is coming to avenge his afflicted followers, the Bridegroom who is coming to consummate his eternal love for his bride, the Judge who will expose everything hidden in darkness, and the Resurrecting One who will make our bodies and all things new.

Even when the focus of a particular sermon or Sunday-school lesson isn't on the return of Christ, you can still show up to church ready to unite with the people of God in believing the promises of God. Simple affirmations in worship songs such as "great is Thy faithfulness" or communal exhortations to "turn your eyes upon Jesus" bind us in our broad trust that God will fulfill all of his promises. When we hear preaching or teaching on promises such as "I am with you always, to the end of the age" (Matt. 28:20), it tilts our momentum toward the promised land and quiets thoughts of returning to Egypt.

Every emphasis on Christ—in whom "all the promises of God find their Yes" (2 Cor. 1:20)—is a reminder that God always keeps his promises and that we can trust him through the wilderness journey.

Hand-Delivered Encouragement

But this ancient picture of solidarity in hearing God's promises is not simply of a mass of Israelites nodding their heads together or shouting, "Amen!" as Caleb proclaims the promises of God. That may be a starting point, but it isn't where the hope is ultimately built.

The real work happens at the "one another" level. Consider these phrases I've italicized:

- "*Exhort one another* every day, as long as it is called 'today,' that none of you may be hardened by the deceitfulness of sin" (Heb. 3:13).
- "And let us consider how to *stir up one another to love and good works*, not neglecting to meet together, as is the habit of some, but *encouraging one another*, and all the more as you see the Day drawing near" (Heb. 10:24–25).

What relationships are needed in our gatherings for this kind of one-anothering to happen?

In Hebrews 3, the author calls us each to start with our own need for such specified attention: "Take care, brothers, lest there be in any of you an evil, unbelieving heart, leading you to fall away from the living God" (Heb. 3:12). What is that area of unbelief in your heart that, if left unattended, could grow into something bigger, even a departure from God altogether? Perhaps it is envy or lust. Maybe you nurture anxious thoughts or doubt that God truly loves you. Perhaps you feel the strong pull to compromise spiritually for the sake of wealth or power. Whether these areas of unbelief spring from a sinful heart, wounds you carry from abuse or neglect, or some combination of the two, they need attention before they steer your life away from God.

This raises crucial questions. Where in your experience of church life will these things be addressed? Will you ask for prayer ministry during the worship service? Are you close enough with your Sunday-school class that you would bring it up with them? Do you have a mentor or close friend you trust enough to disclose your struggle?

Each of us must ask ourselves, "In what relationship can I expose threats to my hope?"

If your church has a mentoring or small-group structure, that might get you closer to this kind of relationship. But even there you need to move toward others who can provide care (and be open to providing that care when others move toward you). This happens as you disclose a generic need for support and gauge whether that person tries to hurriedly fix you with some Christian cliches or shows commitment to pointing you to hope in Christ with patience and gentleness. As trust builds, you can gradually disclose the nature of the threats to your hope and seek solidarity in hearing the promises of God together. Developing such relationships can be long and frustrating work. But weaving our lives together in this way creates a strong fabric of endurance.

What exactly happens in these "one another" relationships?

Hebrews 10:24 addresses this question from the perspective of the one initiating the relationship and, though it is not immediately obvious in the English translation, uses strong language to describe the dynamic: "Let us consider how to stir up one another to love and good works." The call to "consider" is proactive. Driven by a deep concern, it doesn't wait for a request for help but checks in and follows up. This focused attention aims to stir up love and good works. The word translated "stir up" is intense, used negatively to describe the "sharp disagreement" between Paul and Barnabas in Acts 15:39. Here in Hebrews 10:24, various Bible translators render it "spur on," "motivate," "provoke," and "stimulate." This is no pat on the back. This is a fever-pitched, relentless, Caleb-level call to embrace the promises of God and see the deceitfulness of sin. The promised land is at stake! Death in the wilderness is the consequence for disobedience! The choices your brother or sister in Christ makes matter! This is not a call to legalism or fearmongering but a willingness to take seriously the consequences of our daily decisions of where we set our hope. None of us wants to have the testimony of Demas—abandoning the fellowship of those who hold fast to Christ and his promises because we are "in love with this present world" (2 Tim. 4:10).

Church Discipline

When we allow this seriousness to sink in, the next component of church life we will explore, church discipline, should make sense.

In 1 Corinthians 5, Paul addresses a situation of egregious sexual sin in the church—"A man has his father's wife" (v. 1). Even worse, rather than confronting this open immorality, "of a kind that is not tolerated even among pagans," the church is arrogant! Paul tells them what they ought to do: mourn and remove the offender from their church (v. 2).

As he gives these directives, Paul has his sights set on one final, climactic moment: Jesus' return.

"When you are assembled in the name of the Lord Jesus and my spirit is present, with the power of our Lord Jesus, you are to deliver this man to Satan for the destruction of the flesh, so that his spirit may be saved in the day of the Lord" (vv. 4–5).

The future return of Jesus as Judge transforms how Paul approaches present sin in the church. His command "to deliver this man to Satan" (v. 5) is parallel to his instruction in verse 2: "Let him who has done this be removed from among you." By excommunicating the offender from the fellowship of God's people, Paul wants to remove this man's presumption of enjoying reconciled fellowship with God. Paul may be referencing the first Passover on the eve of the Hebrew slaves' exodus from Egypt.[33] Like a firstborn son removed from the home where the blood of the Passover lamb covers the doorpost, this one is to feel exposed to the destroyer and run back home for spiritual protection.

While there are many exegetical and practical details that could be addressed from this text, the larger takeaway is how church discipline is tethered to the day of the Lord. Much more than an obsolete or antiquated practice, this is the natural outworking of a life of hearing God's promises together and applying them to one another specifically. Hebrews 3 warns us to listen to God's promises, exhort one another daily, and "hold our original confidence firm to the end" (vv. 12–14) so that we do not become like those Israelites "whose bodies fell in the wilderness" (v. 17), to whom God swore, "They shall not enter my rest" (v. 11).

At stake in this is judgment.

And thus as God's people who belong to the age to come yet still live in this present age, we are to take steps of judgment now that will avert condemnation at the coming of the Judge. Notice that Paul addresses the whole congregation in 1 Corinthians 5, not only the leaders. This falls in line with Jesus' original instructions about church discipline in Matthew 18: "If your brother sins against you, go and tell him his fault, between you and him alone" (v. 15). Only after repeated pleas for repentance with an expanding circle of witnesses is this to be carried to the whole church. If the offender refuses to listen, he is to be treated as an unbeliever (v. 17).

Do you see the organic progression here between this and our previous two points? You gather with other believers to nurture solidarity with those who listen to God's promises. In that context, you have the opportunity to stir up and be stirred up by others toward love and good works. But let's say that one of your fellow church members begins living in clear disobedience to the way of Jesus, disregarding the promises of God and embracing the promises of sin. You continue the "one anothering" work. You doggedly pursue them, reminding them of God's promises like Caleb pointing to God's delight and deliverance. You listen. You pray. You spend time together. You model faithfulness to Jesus.

But if, over time, that person continues in unrepentant disobedience, you must ask for help from a few other mature believers to "[bring] back a sinner from his wandering" (James 5:20) and "restore such a person with a gentle spirit" (Gal. 6:1 CSB). And if the person refuses to turn back from their sinful trajectory and return to faithful obedience to Jesus, they are to be put out of the church.

What drives all of this is "so that his spirit may be saved in the day of the Lord" (1 Cor. 5:5). Sin in the church—tragic and unwelcome as it is—forces us to question whether we truly believe that Jesus is Lord, whether we truly believe that he will return as Judge. The aim of this extreme but necessary step of church discipline is to affirm our conviction that the coming judgment is real and to plead with the one who is straying to return to Christ and again be united with those who listen to his promises.[34]

This process played out in real time for one man who wrote about his story of living a double life—faithfully attending church and playing on the worship team while engaging in unbridled sexual immorality. After being excommunicated by his church and, years later, walking through a restoration process, he testified, "To this day, I don't know if I was a backslidden convert or if I was a deceived non-Christian.

Either way, church discipline served to expose my hypocrisy. It forced me to deal with the claims of Christ. God used membership and exclusion to show me that life in the world without God is miserable, and my only hope is Christ."[35]

The Lord's Supper

A fourth way our gathering nurtures a love for Jesus' appearing is through taking the Lord's Supper.

The judgment Paul pronounced and called the church to enact on the sexually immoral man in 1 Corinthians 5 was of a piece with the judgment the Corinthians were already experiencing. In chapter 11 of the same letter, Paul writes that "many of you are weak and ill, and some have died" because they were taking the Lord's Supper "in an unworthy manner" (1 Cor. 11:27, 30). The description of how they were going about the meal suggests that the wealthy hosts accentuated the existing divisions of wealth and class in how they celebrated the meal. The wealthy feasted luxuriously in the VIP room while the working-class members crammed into the peanut gallery, eating the leftovers. This was antithetical to their unity and equality in Christ, which Paul unpacks in the following chapters through the metaphor of the body (1 Corinthians 12–14).

What are we to make of this judgment?

This judgment—which Paul is careful to identify as God's discipline, not eternal condemnation (1 Cor. 11:32)—reminds us yet again that the life of the church in the present is thoroughly connected to our shared, glorious future. We are not a civic organization or a nonprofit charity but the eternal family of God. And nowhere was this made more explicit than in the way Jesus instituted the Lord's Supper.

Our Lord inaugurated this meal while he and the disciples were eating the Passover meal. The Gospels don't walk through each step of the meal (for instance, when the youngest child in attendance asked, "Why is tonight different from all other nights?"), but the account of Jesus' taking the bread and the cup fits perfectly within the meal's framework of the roasted lamb, bitter herbs, recounting of the exodus, and singing of the psalms of praise.

Most significant, there were four cups of wine involved in the Passover meal. Based on where the bread was in the meal, it is most likely that the cup Jesus passed around for the disciples to drink from was the third cup. This adds a poignancy to the words he speaks next: "Truly, I say to you, I will not drink again of the fruit of the vine until that day when I drink it new in the kingdom of God" (Mark 14:25). He did not finish the Passover meal. He left the fourth cup. The first Lord's Supper was an incomplete meal.

This incomplete meal sets up the expectation for when Jesus will eat it again.

Paul captures this dynamic in 1 Corinthians 11. After reminding the church of Jesus' words surrounding the bread and the cup, Paul places this gospel meal in its redemptive historical context: "For as often as you eat this bread and drink the cup, you proclaim the Lord's death until he comes" (v. 26).

When you take the Lord's Supper, you are looking both backward and forward. You are looking backward at the cross, proclaiming that Christ died for our sins. You are, to borrow Paul's word from 1 Corinthians 10:16, participating in the body and blood of Christ. His body was broken for sins you committed, his blood shed to forgive your rebellion. In eating the communion elements, you share the benefits of what Christ accomplished freely, graciously, lovingly on your behalf. It is a freedom meal where the price of your release is soberly and gladly celebrated.

Yet this backward look at Christ's death for us anticipates the day when Christ will again eat the meal with us. By faith we feast on Christ now—spiritually, not literally—but we do this only "until he comes." When he returns, his promise from the Gospels will be fulfilled. He will pick up the fourth cup and drink it, with resurrection newness, in the consummated kingdom of God. We experience the presence of Christ now through the indwelling Holy Spirit. But this is only a foretaste of our taking the meal with the one who loved us and gave himself for us.

Revelation portrays this as a wedding feast, "the marriage supper of the Lamb" (Rev. 19:9). The image is of holy joy, intimacy, and celebration. There we will know a union with Christ beyond our deepest attachments on earth. There our participation in Christ will reach a crescendo of delight. There we will feast forever.

So you can take the bread and the cup in hope. You proclaim the Lord's death until he returns. You feast on Christ in anticipation of feasting with Christ. Ask the Spirit to grant you the sanctified imagination to see yourself feasting with the Bridegroom. Eat the bit of bread and sip from the cup as the hors d'oeuvres to that great meal to come.

Church life is meant to nurture our anticipation of Jesus' return. As I think about how this has played out in my life, what has changed me is not an institution but the people who make up that institution. I think of the preachers whose exposition of God's Word beautified the promises of God and helped me detox from the allurements of acclaim, comfort, and sensuality. I think of friends and mentors who have called me out when they have seen my life going in a sinful direction. I think of the accountability partners to whom I have exposed threats to my hope.

My prayer for you is not only that you would find a healthy church where you can have this kind of spiritual support but also that you would be the Caleb whom someone else needs, the one reminding them that God always keeps his promises. May you encourage other believers in your context, and all the more as you see the day of Jesus' return drawing near.

Questions for Reflection

1. Did you bring any disillusionment with the church into reading this chapter? If so, reflect on the yearnings for Christian fellowship you feel after reading it.
2. How might the pursuit of hope in Jesus' return change how you listen to sermons or Sunday-school lessons?

3. In what relationships can you disclose the sin that threatens your hope? If you do not have such a relationship now, what is a next step you can take to developing that with a trusted believer?

4. Have you ever confronted someone about their sin? How was your admonition received? Based on what we saw in the examples of Caleb and the Corinthian church, would you do anything differently?

5. Jesus promised that he would eat the Lord's Supper "new in the kingdom of God" (Mark 14:25). How can meditating on this promise help you anticipate Jesus' return when you take communion?

CHAPTER 9

FAST

"Daddy, the dog is missing!"

Those are never words you want to wake up to, but they're the ones my son spoke into my Sunday afternoon nap.

I am a deep sleeper and slow to get cracking. But when this message reached my brain, it jolted me awake so that within minutes I was dressed, adrenaline pumping, on my way to find the missing dog.

Time was of the essence, so I didn't brush my teeth, comb my hair, or see whether my clothes matched. I may have looked like a mess as I slowly prowled around our neighborhood in our old car, but that was irrelevant. Our Westie, older than all of our children, was missing and we were on high alert while we looked for him. As my chest pounded, I inhabited that mental space of being simultaneous scattered—since he could be anywhere—and laser focused on finding our dog.

This is the level of intensity we described in chapter 5 about Jesus' return as the Bridegroom. When we left the story, the smoke was clearing and the dust was settling from the hole in the wall left by the black SUV. The joyous wedding had been brought to a shocking halt when the Bridegroom was extracted. Now we blink our eyes to take in this traumatic, adrenaline-fueled moment. There is nothing normal about it. Before the narrator could finish "and they all lived happily . . ." the hero of the story was taken away.

None of this suggests that these events were unanticipated by Jesus and his Father. The disciples were given ample heads-up. It simply situates where *we* are in the drama. The Lover of our souls came in person, made the greatest sacrifice possible, and returned to his people alive and new. They were together, there at the altar. And now he is gone.

Imagine yourself in the wedding scene as the smoke clears and the dust settles. You can feel your heart beating in your chest and your mind racing a mile a minute. You are disoriented, confused, heartbroken. In your peripheral vision, someone approaches. It's your uncle James. He's holding something in his hand. As your eyes struggle to focus, you realize he's carrying a tray of food from the reception hall. "Meatball?" he asks.

Like most people, you would respond, exasperated, "How can you eat at a time like this?"

This is the moment we want to capture in our fasting. Not the confusion or dismay but the longing, the aching, the single-minded yearning to be with the one who loves us. Because we are not a cousin or best friend or grandparent in this wedding party. We are the bride, and our Bridegroom has been taken before we even made it to the honeymoon. And the single desire of our hearts is to be with him again.

As Jesus himself predicted, "The days will come when

the bridegroom is taken away from them, and then they will fast" (Matt. 9:15).

A Hunger to be with Jesus Again

Of course, even though Uncle James jumped the gun on the meatballs, you do have to eat eventually, right? Such is the nature of adrenaline—it has to subside at some point. After I spent forty-five minutes searching our neighborhood for the lost dog, I had to take a break and collect my thoughts.

Unlike me in my search for the dog, we know where Jesus is. After he was lifted into heaven, two men in white robes, presumably angels, asked the disciples, "Men of Galilee, why do you stand looking into heaven? This Jesus, who was taken up from you into heaven, will come in the same way as you saw him go into heaven" (Acts 1:11). As the rest of Acts bears out, the disciples' next steps were to do the last thing Jesus told them to do—"Be my witnesses" from their back yard to the ends of the earth (v. 8). And as they did, they continued to fast as an expression of their hunger to be with Jesus again.

In this chapter we will walk through three questions about fasting: Why do we fast? From what do we fast? How do we fast? This will not be a comprehensive study of fasting in the Bible,[36] but because Jesus' words about our fasting for the Bridegroom are so brief, we will rely on other Scripture passages to give us direction.

Why Should We Fast?

Why fast? One answer is that Jesus assumes we will fast. We have already seen his words in Matthew 9: "Then they will fast." In the Sermon on the Mount, Jesus assumes this as well. He doesn't say "if you fast" but "when you fast" (Matt. 6:16), alongside his teaching on praying and giving to the needy. It is not an imperative with the same strength as "repent and believe in the gospel" (Mark 1:15), but it is something Jesus assumes will be part of his disciples' lives.

But beyond that assumption, why do we fast? In the Matthew 9 passage, Jesus says it is because the Bridegroom was taken away. Then, without changing the subject, he says, "No one puts a piece of unshrunk cloth on an old garment, for the patch tears away from the garment, and a worse tear is made. Neither is new wine put into old wineskins. If it is, the skins burst and the wine is spilled and the skins are destroyed. But new wine is put into fresh wineskins, and so both are preserved" (Matt. 9:16–17).

Jesus himself transforms fasting. As Israel's longed-for Messiah, the Bridegroom of God's people, Jesus' very presence is a party. He is a cause to feast. And on the flip side, his absence is a reason to fast.

This is not to say that the reasons God's people fasted in past centuries are now inappropriate, only that they now find their focus in the simple fact that the Bridegroom was taken away and we now long for his presence. The "fresh wineskins" of fasting is a yearning for Christ's return.

Let's apply this to two very different situations in which we find ourselves.

Why fast? Because *Jesus is gone and life is hard*.

Difficult times have a way of putting blinders on you. Sickness, depression, financial strain, and broken relationships all can dim your sense of hope. We know the big-picture resolution will come when Jesus returns to make all things new, when the Bridegroom returns for his bride. But when things are difficult, we are prone to lose sight of that. So we need help.

In such times it is easy to anesthetize the hardship with something accessible like scrolling through social media, playing a mindless video game, or binge watching a TV show. Then there are less innocuous ways to numb ourselves, such as alcohol, pornography, cutting, or compulsive spending. But these don't heal. They may temporarily calm nerves and dull pain, but they can never renew hope.

As counterintuitive as it sounds, in hard times we actually need to create more space to nurture a love for Jesus' appearing, space to recognize our pain and longing rather than numb or ignore it. We see in the Old Testament stories of Esther and Jehoshaphat and Ezra that it was in desperate times that God's people fasted, realizing they needed to intensify their dependence on God. There is a time when you need to laugh and blow off steam and be silly. But there is also a time when you need to strip down your schedule to the bare bones and seek God with all your attention. Life is hard, and we must connect with how the story ends at Christ's return—the creation made new, eternity in the presence of God, every tear wiped away, and every sad thing made untrue. Fasting connects us with that hope in such a way that the Holy Spirit gives us joy, peace, and rest in the presence of God now.

But we also fast for the opposite reason: because *Jesus is gone and life is good*.

We go through seasons of difficulty, and we go through seasons of ease. Perhaps right now you have some financial padding, your health is strong, and everybody is happy. Life is good.

If you are in a season like that right now, I'm not here to rain on your parade. Be grateful! Count your blessings! And beware. It is one thing to enjoy the good gifts of God; it is another to love the gifts such that you no longer love the Giver. In Proverbs 30:9, the author prays that God will not make him wealthy, "lest I be full and deny you and say, 'Who is the LORD?'"

We see this modeled in Daniel's life. During the Babylonian captivity, Daniel was one of an elite group of promising young Judeans—the Rhodes Scholars of his day—to be handpicked by King Nebuchadnezzar's chief of staff for education in Babylon. He was given a new Babylonian name honoring the god Bel and granted a portion of food from the king's own table. From an academic standpoint, this was like hitting the jackpot. The Neo-Babylonian Empire reigned supreme, and Daniel was elevated immediately to its upper echelon of power. But from a spiritual perspective, this opportunity was highly dangerous. Daniel held allegiance to Yahweh, not Bel or Aku or Marduk. The Babylonian goal was to assimilate this sharp young man entirely into its culture, and Daniel's goal was to resist. So how would he retain his faithfulness in a foreign land?

In a surprising decision, the area where Daniel pushed back was not in being renamed after a false god or studying the Babylonian magical arts, like astrology or examining sheep livers to predict future events. Rather, he drew the line at the food. He requested only vegetables and water.

What makes this account fascinating is that Daniel does not seem to have made this decision based purely on the Torah's restriction against eating certain meats. If that were the only restriction, he wouldn't have refused the wine from the king's table. But "Daniel resolved that he would not defile himself with the king's food, or with the wine that he drank" (Dan. 1:8), not only for kosher concerns but also for the sake of his spiritual identity. He didn't want to be lulled into spiritual apathy by the luxury of the king's cuisine. So he and his close friends committed themselves to a form of fasting that would keep them dependent on Yahweh to grant them physical and academic success.

In the same way, we fast when life is good not because we are ascetics who have renounced pleasure in this world but because we are easily deluded to believe that the good things of this life will last forever. So our enjoyment of good things should be mingled with remembering the best things, what is to come. We should both taste the sweetness of abundant food and abstain for a season so that we can acquire a taste for heaven's superior delights. We fast because Jesus our Bridegroom is not here, and no matter how tasty the wedding reception spread may be, life is not complete until we are in the presence of the one who loves us.

What Should We Fast From?

What should we abstain from when we fast?

The Scriptures contain a number of examples.

One is to fast from *all food*. This is normative fasting in the Bible—fasting from all food for a set period of time. Early Christians fasted two days a week, while Jesus launched his ministry with a forty-day fast. There was a set period of time to abstain from eating.

Another is to fast from *some food*. We saw this in the example of Daniel as a young man. Later in his life, he would initiate a similar partial fast. "I, Daniel, was mourning for three weeks. I ate no delicacies, no meat or wine entered my mouth, nor did I anoint myself at all, for the full three weeks" (Dan. 10:2–3). In a New Testament parallel to the limited diet many of the prophets had, John the Baptist ate only wild locust and honey. So in this form of fasting, there is a longer period of time—weeks, months, even years—of eating a limited diet.

If you have a difficult relationship with food, whether medically or emotionally, please include conversations with your medical professional or counselor in your consideration of fasting from food. You may decide that you want to focus on the next category instead of exacerbating other challenges.

To broaden things, we can fast from *anything good but distracting.*

To discern what might fit into this category, let's remember why we're fasting in the first place. Jesus our Bridegroom is gone. He's been whisked away from the wedding, and we long for him to come back so we can be with him forever. Fasting is our means of nurturing a love for Jesus' appearing. So think about your life and consider: What activities distract you from hoping fully in Jesus' return? It could be the sitcoms or standup comedy you watch, the social media world you've created, the podcasts you listen to, the political news and punditry you follow, the fiction you read, the video games you play, sports that you participate in or watch, or a hobby like woodworking or flying radio-controlled planes. I could go on forever, because there are an infinite number of good things to do in this life that can distract you from the best thing. Think of it as fasting from the American dream to long for heaven's King.

If this category feels like playing fast and loose with fasting, think about the radically different kind of world we live in now compared with previous generations. I am not categorically old (unless you ask my children), but in my lifetime I have seen how we watch TV and movies at home transition from "if you missed it you missed it" to the introduction of VHS tapes to DVR to streaming services. We now live in an on-demand world where the TV doesn't go static at midnight and you can consume whatever entertainment you want when you want. Not only is this available at any time, it is also accessible at any place. Now we carry our distraction devices with us in our pockets, rather than having to go to a theater or a room in the house to be diverted. Layer on social media and you can chat with anyone in the world about what piques your interest.

Our propensity to distract ourselves, which has existed

for millennia, now has limitless options for keeping our attention from the most important things. While I think fasting from food is still an important discipline, I also believe a retreat from the 24/7 availability of entertainment and sports and news can situate our hearts to long for what matters most. Step out of the data stream and bask in the sunlight of God's presence.

How Should We Fast?

This segues into our third question: How? How should we fast?

When I was scouring my neighborhood for our runaway dog, the method of my pursuit was secondary to its aim: finding the dog! Once I took a few minutes to sit down, catch my breath, and pray, I thought of putting the word out on Nextdoor, a neighborhood-based social network. Within five minutes, a neighbor around the corner called me to let me know that Sinclair was hanging out in their back yard. Relief and joy flooded my heart. I celebrated with my wife and kids. When I brought our goofy, curious, slightly naughty dog back, it was a sweet reunion as everyone took a turn welcoming him home with hugs and belly rubs.

Fasting exists as a means to an end, like a date exists to spend time with your husband or public transportation exists to get you to work. So in the Sermon on the Mount, Jesus reminds us that we fast not for fasting's sake, and certainly not to bring attention to ourselves, but *for God*. "And when you fast, do not look gloomy like the hypocrites, for they disfigure their faces that their fasting may be seen by others. Truly, I say to you, they have received their reward. But when you fast, anoint your head and wash your face, that your fasting may not be seen by others but by your Father who is in secret. And your Father who sees in secret will reward you" (Matt. 6:16–18).

If you are new to fasting, don't let fasting itself become the focus. Use it as a means to an end. Give as much attention to what you will do as to what you will not do. Once you've decided on that meal or that screen time or the hobby you will forego, pray about what you will do instead that will further shape your life around Jesus' return.

Here are some suggestions:

- Read the entire New Testament in three months, paying careful attention to the mentions of Christ's return.
- Create and listen to a playlist of worship songs that highlight Jesus' coming.
- Pray for God to save lost friends and family members before that final day.
- Incorporate your time of encouraging one another (from chap. 8) through prayer for and checking in with struggling believers.
- Practice sitting still before the Lord and imagining how everything will change the moment you see Jesus.

Start somewhere, and trust God to build this new practice of fasting into the rhythm of your week.

How do we fast? For God. But also, we fast *with others*.

This probably sounds contradictory. But just because we don't fast to be seen by others doesn't mean we can't fast with others.

Most of the fasts in the Old Testament were communal. When King Jehoshaphat "set his face to seek the LORD" as enemy armies descended on Jerusalem, he "proclaimed a fast throughout all Judah" (2 Chron. 20:3). Ezra proclaimed a fast for all the exiles returning to Jerusalem, imploring them to cry out to God for a safe journey. Esther called for all of the Jews in Susa to fast for the three days leading up to her bold request to the king to save her people. Likewise, the fasts recorded in the book of Acts were part of corporate worship (13:2–3) and church planting (14:23).

This is not to discourage personal fasting. In the examples we saw from Daniel, one was with his friends and the other by himself. Nehemiah also reports fasting individually (Neh. 1:4). And, of course, Jesus fasted by himself at the outset of his ministry.

But if you find yourself struggling to grow in your anticipation of Jesus' return through fasting, consider asking others to fast and pray with you. Some of the wisest advice I received as a young believer was to turn my weaknesses into opportunities for community. I was told, "If you don't read the Bible enough, start a Bible study. If you don't pray enough, start a prayer group." And to that I add, "If you don't find yourself yearning for the Lord's return, ask someone to fast and pray with you."

One of the seasons of greatest growth in my faith came

during my junior and senior years of college. A dear brother and I committed to skipping lunch to pray for an hour once per week. During those times in an austere, ten-by-ten dorm room, it was as if we entered the gates of heaven and bowed at the very throne of God. We had no agenda, no prayer list, only the priority of worship, adoration, and luxuriating in the presence of God. I have had such prayer times by myself, but something about praying with someone with shared zeal exponentially enhances the experience.

No pleasure on this earth can match the pleasure of being in the presence of the Bridegroom, of basking in his covenant love for you. Remove obstacles and ask for whatever help you need to be rooted and grounded in his love, poised to anticipate his return more than any other event.

Questions for Reflection

1. What are two good things and two hard things that have diminished your anticipation of Jesus' return?
2. If you do not currently fast, from what do you think you should fast to nurture a love for Jesus' appearing?
3. What do you plan to do when you are fasting? It could be something from pages 139–41 or something else God leads you to do.
4. Who can you tell about your fasting plan—someone who can both encourage you and provide perspective if you find the venture challenging?

CHAPTER 10

REST

I see the Sabbath as practicing for eternity. The weekly cycle of work and rest is a microcosm of this life preparing for our final rest with God. You work and work and work throughout the week, then you make preparations to rest. You get your space ready, prepare food ahead of time, and arrange everything so that, for those twenty-four hours, it is nothing but enjoyment of God and his good gifts."

My dad shared this insight with my wife during a family visit in 2017. Six months later he died unexpectedly of a heart attack. When you lose someone in such a shocking way, you tend to dig for those recent conversations like you are mining for gold. But I cherish his words not only because of their proximity to his death but also because of how true they proved in a poignant, if painful, way. Dad was practicing for heaven, and now he is there. He is no longer bound to the world of heart disease, flooded basements, political disagreement, Alzheimer's, and broken transmissions. He is now in the presence of God, breathing the atmosphere of heaven, caught up in eternal worship, submerged in divine love.

Think of all the excuses we give for why taking a weekly day of rest is untenable for our schedules—all the things we have to do, the busyness at work, the demands of family. There is enough to do in this world to keep one busy every second of their life. But one day none of these things will hold sway over us anymore. So why do we allow the priorities of this passing life to hold us back from the pleasures of the life to come, the life that has already broken into our world through Christ and the Spirit?

I have two proposals to make in this chapter: First, we anticipate a final Sabbath that Jesus will bring about at his return. In the words of Hebrews 4:9, "there remains a Sabbath rest for the people of God." And second, we increase this anticipation through practicing that Sabbath rest each week.

We will explore this by looking at the story of rest in the biblical narrative and the practice of rest in real time. Of the three rhythms, this is the least explicitly tied to the return of Christ in the New Testament. Plus, theological views abound regarding how we should relate to the Sabbath now. My interest is not to weigh in on those debates. My dad and I did not agree on many of those surrounding issues. But we found common ground in viewing the Sabbath as a gift, as Jesus implied when he said that "the Sabbath was made to meet the needs of people" (Mark 2:27 NLT).

I pray you will receive this gift and, through it, increase in your yearning for the final rest Jesus will bring about at his appearing.[37]

The Story of Rest

We are going to use Hebrews 4 as a launching point to tell this story. I will only reference the text here, but if you want to get the full effect, take a minute to read the whole chapter. (It's only sixteen verses—shouldn't take long.)

Hebrews 4 identifies three points of rest on the timeline of redemptive history. Each is associated with the land where God dwelled with his people. The first is *the garden of Eden.* Hebrews 4:4 says that on the seventh day of creation, God rested from all his works. This is a quote from Genesis 2, which goes on to say that "God blessed the seventh day and made it holy" (Gen. 2:3).

God built Sabbath rest into the creation. After a six-day workweek in which he formed and filled the world, God created something on the seventh day by his inactivity. He set apart and blessed this day as a time to behold and enjoy the very good work he had done. To be clear, God did not rest because he was tired. He did not cease from his work because his back was sore from making the solar system or because he pulled a hamstring while creating the hippopotamus. He is God. He created light from darkness, order from chaos, something from nothing with an effortless, almighty word.

No, God paused from his work because the point of work is not work. The point of God's work is to enjoy how his work displays his glory. This is God's rest. When he sabbathed for the first time, God stepped back from his handiwork, saw what he had made, and smiled with delight and joy. "Very good," he said. Perhaps you have done this after cleaning the kitchen. You take a moment to survey your work, feel the inner calm, relish the order, and take in the good work you've done. I do this with my teenaged sons when they mow the lawn. I step outside, put my arms around their shoulders, breathe in the smell of freshly cut grass, and invite them to admire their excellent work.

These are echoes of what took place on the seventh day. God took in the goodness of what he had made and welcomed the man and woman into this enjoyment. This is the climax of the creation week—God's rest.

The next reference to rest in Hebrews 4 is that of *the promised land*. In chapter 8 we heard the cautionary tale of the freed Israelite slaves from Hebrews 3. Their pining for Egyptian cucumbers and their fear of the giants in the promised land choked out any faith they had in Yahweh's ability to make good on his promise. They died in unbelief.

But as we see in Hebrews 4:8, Joshua led the next generation into the promised land. And the promise of this inheritance was not only of land but of rest in that land: "Rest from all your enemies" (Deut. 12:10; 25:19). In many ways, the promised land had parallel significance to the garden of Eden. Adam and Eve did nothing to build the garden. They simply received it and were charged by God to cultivate it and enjoy it. In the same way, God gave Israel the promised land: "great and good cities that you did not build, and houses full of all good things that you did not fill, and cisterns that you did not dig, and vineyards and olive trees that you did not plant" (Deut. 6:10–11). They received it as grace. And as grace, they were to cultivate it for six days a week, then pause to enjoy it on the seventh. Great detail accompanied the command for Sabbath observance in the law of Moses, such that we might see the command as a burden. But we must not lose sight of the purpose of the command: to shape Israel's experience of the land as a place where they could flourish, delight in God, and enjoy his good gifts.

But that did not fully happen. They didn't fully drive out their enemies. They didn't fully trust in Yahweh and obey his commands. They lived in the promised land but did not enter his rest. Hebrews 4:8–9 tells us, "If Joshua had given them rest, God would not have spoken of another day later on. So then, there remains a Sabbath rest for the people of God." This was true of the church two thousand years ago, and it is true of us now. This chapter will explore how to practice rest now because we live in an era when rest is not our natural state.

The final rest we anticipate is the third point on the timeline, and it is still in the future: the new Jerusalem. The writer doesn't mention it in Hebrews 4, but later in chapters 11–13, he will speak of the heavenly city God has prepared for those who trust him: "Mount Zion . . . the city of the living God, the heavenly Jerusalem" (Heb. 12:22), "the city that is to come" (13:14). Now we, the church, are that people trekking through the wilderness, facing temptations that distract our focus from Jesus. Like Joshua and Caleb, we must encourage one another, remind one another of God's superior power and promises, and keep on the path to our final Sabbath rest.

And how do we keep on that path? By faith. "We who have believed enter that rest" (Heb. 4:3). The path to the new Jerusalem begins now by trusting in Jesus who said, "Come to me, all who labor and are heavy laden, and I will give you rest" (Matt. 11:28).

Believer in Christ, there remains a Sabbath rest for the people of God. It is found in Jesus, who promises rest for our souls and rest in the new Jerusalem. As we read in the final chapters of Revelation, there will be nothing false or unclean in this city, neither mourning nor crying nor pain. It will be the place where God dwells with his people and we with our God. No striving, no surviving, but dwelling. Like the garden of Eden and the promised land, this will be a place we do not build, but rather a place God has built for us. We will walk the streets of gold he has paved, live in one of the many rooms he has prepared, and behold the jewel-encrusted walls he has constructed as they reflect in technicolor the brilliance of our King. This will be an eternity of rest, of play, of worshiping and cultivating and exploring and fellowshiping and telling of the mighty victory our Savior has wrought for us. We who have rested in Jesus will, perfectly and eternally, enter God's rest.

This is our home. This is the earth the meek will inherit when Jesus returns to make all things new. It is the shalom-saturated society Jesus will bring about when he sets all things right. It is your greatest vacation multiplied by your redeemed vocation, raised exponentially to the power of eternity. This is our hope, our inheritance at the return of Christ.

The Practice of Rest

How do we nurture anticipation for that day? How do we get a taste of a home in which we have not yet dwelled? By practicing Sabbath rest now. As we saw in Hebrews 4:3, it is those who believe the gospel who enter this rest. So we practice Sabbath rest first and foremost by trusting in Jesus to save us.

The Jesus who saves us had a lot to say about the way the Sabbath had been turned into a legalistic burden for the people of God. "The Sabbath was made for man," Jesus told the Pharisees, "not man for the Sabbath" (Mark 2:27). He performed miracles on the Sabbath, flashing glimpses of new creation. He initiated a transformation of the Sabbath that his servant Paul continued when he challenged Christians in Colossae to "let no one pass judgment on you in questions of . . . [the] Sabbath" (Col. 2:16) and told the believers in Rome, "One person esteems one day as better than another, while another esteems all days alike. Each one should be fully convinced in his own mind" (Rom. 14:5).

So our practice of Sabbath has radically transformed since the days of Israel in the wilderness. It centers on trust in Christ rather than strict adherence to the law. Yet the heart of this rest remains the same, going all the way back to God's seventh-day rest at the climax of his creation week. Let me suggest three ways we enter God's rest and anticipate our eternal rest that Jesus will bring about when he returns to make all things new.

Rest to Anticipate the Redemption of Work

Work was one of the first casualties of the fall. Rather than tending and keeping God's good, fertile land in Eden, our first parents were consigned to cultivate food from a ground that also produced thorns and thistles. They could bring new life into the world only in bodies that felt the pain of childbirth. Because of their sin, the sweat of the brow and the desperate labor for survival replace the delightful, creative endeavor that once was work (Gen. 3:16–19). A thousand ills have accompanied this state of affairs, from unjustly hoarding the fruit of our labor, to becoming enslaved to work, to finding our identity in our work rather than in our relationship with God.

When Jesus returns, he will come to "make his blessings known far as the curse is found."[38] Not only will we receive new bodies that will no longer sweat and groan but "the creation itself"—now in the pains of childbirth—"will be set free from its bondage to corruption and obtain the freedom of the glory of the children of God" (Rom. 8:21). We will no longer work because we have to but because we get to. Surviving will be replaced by thriving in the new Jerusalem, where fruit grows with ease and abundance surpasses that of Eden.

So when we practice rest now, we anticipate the redemption of work Jesus will bring about at his coming. For twenty-four hours each week, we cease from survival and partake of a foretaste of plenty.

What does this look like?

The first step is simply to stop working. Cease from your labor for a twenty-four-hour period. This will be more challenging for some than others, but the goal is to create space in your week where you can pause all your paid and unpaid work—doing your job, paying bills, doing chores, and so on. Take a break from the thorns and thistles.

This raises a question: What is work? I don't mean that in a philosophical sense; quite the opposite. In the most concrete way possible, ask whether the things you do each week fall under "I have to do this" or "I get to do this." My email account lies dormant when I Sabbath, but I delight in taking my youngest child to the park and watching a movie with my family. Part of the work my wife does is planning and preparing meals each day. So when she practices Sabbath, she rests from food preparation. Usually this requires ensuring that we have enough leftovers or snack foods to feed our family for a day. That work happens during the days before Sabbath so she is released from that labor.

In general, it is wise to shape your day of rest around the gathering of God's people on the Lord's Day. Just as the Jewish Sabbath (Shabbat) begins at sundown before their gathered worship, pausing to rest at sundown on Saturday evening can set you up to maximize your experience of meeting together on Sunday to hear God's promises, encourage one another, and take the Lord's Supper, "all the more as you see the Day drawing near" (Heb. 10:25).

As a pastor, making Sunday my day of rest does not work well for me. Jesus even points out that "the priests in the temple profane the Sabbath and are guiltless" (Matt. 12:5). So I take Fridays off from my work at the church and the to-do list at home. Again, Sabbath rest is a gift, not a restriction, so feel the joy of flexibility even as you commit yourself to ceasing from labor once per week.

As you do so, luxuriate in the idea of living in a resurrected creation where soil and tree and fruit will comprise the landscape and where the cultivation of our sustenance will be a beautiful expression of our creativity as image bearers of the Creator rather than a desperate endeavor. There work will be so close to play we may not be able to tell the difference. So spend time on your day of rest enjoying those activities that feel like play, whether it be swinging your child at the park, gardening, woodworking, playing a musical instrument, or editing a home movie. Play and anticipate the joy of an eternity of redeemed work.

Rest to Anticipate God's Eternal Rule

Embedded in the curse was not only the breakdown of work but also the introduction of strife and an imbalance of power. God told the serpent of the enmity it would have with the woman and told Eve, "Your desire shall be contrary to your husband, but he shall rule over you" (Gen. 3:15–16). However you interpret these predictions, the ensuing chapters of Genesis—Cain killing Abel, Abraham calling Sarah his sister, Rebekah and Jacob deceiving Isaac and Esau, Joseph's brothers selling him into slavery—bear out the manipulation and misuse of power that have characterized human families and society until the present day.

Our cries of "Maranatha!" anticipate an end of power plays, one-upmanship, and exploitation. After those who belong to Jesus are resurrected "at his coming . . . then comes the end, when he delivers the kingdom to God the Father after destroying every rule and every authority and power" (1 Cor. 15:23–24). At long last the world will be rid of war. God will be King and all will be at rest.

Sabbath is your weekly opportunity to listen to this news rather than the twenty-four-hour news cycle that reports stories of betrayal, uprisings, murder, and abuse through our ubiquitous screens. Detach, unplug, and tune in to the eternal news story that will play when Jesus returns: "The kingdom of the world has become the kingdom of our Lord and of his Christ, and he shall reign forever and ever" (Rev. 11:15).

This may feel challenging for those who passionately pursue justice in this life. Why not spend every waking moment working for the oppressed? William Wilberforce, the British politician who fought for dozens of just causes, most notably the abolition of slavery in Great Britain, recognized that an incessant labor for good things could both dull his effectiveness and bloat his ego. He saw fellow members of Parliament lose their lives to burnout and their souls to arrogance. His remedy was Sabbath observance. In his journal he wrote, "Blessed be God for the day of rest and religious occupations wherein earthly things assume their true size and ambition is stunted."[39]

Still, this is a lot to ask for those who carry the scars of abuse or cannot turn off the prejudice of others. I'm not suggesting that we bury our heads in the sand to pretend that bad things aren't happening. I am suggesting that our weekly Sabbath serve as a time to zoom out from the immediate injustices of our lives and the world around us to focus on the end of the story when Jesus puts things right. Murderers, the sexually immoral, cowards, and liars will not be part of this new Jerusalem. Rather, God will dwell with his redeemed people once his work of making all things new—including our sin-bent hearts—is finished (Rev. 21:1–8).

A weekly Sabbath invites us to tune in entirely to this final rule of God. One way we can enter this reality is through meditating on the first half of the prayer Jesus taught us. We are to pray, "Our Father in heaven, your name be honored as holy. Your kingdom come. Your will be done on earth as it is in heaven" (Matt. 6:9–13 CSB).

This is, at its essence, a prayer for Christ's return. As such, it can be used as a meditation on what he will bring about at that return. Take time on your Sabbath to ponder a world where God's name—his character, reputation, and renown—is honored as holy. Contemplate the rule of God being complete in the individuals, families, and communities around you. Allow your sanctified imagination to ponder life when God's desires are carried out by everyone on earth with the same immediacy and delight with which they are carried out by those in heaven.

Again, this is not living in denial. It is embracing our conviction that our context of mistreatment, injustice, disregard, and lies will one day come to an end. "Everything in the world—the lust of the flesh, the lust of the eyes, and the pride in one's possessions . . . is passing away, but the one who does the will of God remains forever" (1 John 2:16–17 CSB). When we envision the fulfillment of the Lord's Prayer, we lean into our future and find strength to live under God's rule the other six days of the week.

Rest to Anticipate Eternal Delight

Another tragedy of the fall that continues to this day is the spoiling of delight. Because of their rebellion against God, Adam and Eve's beautiful, intimate relationship of being naked and not ashamed (Gen. 2:25) devolved into one of betrayal and mistrust. Fruit was replaced by thorns and sweet communion with God by the fear of judgment. Like green mold on a fine cheese or white fuzz on once-luscious strawberries, sin ruins delight in God's good gifts.

Thus the vision of heaven revealed to God's people is one of "love's purest joys restored."[40] The gates of the new Jerusalem are made of pearl, its streets paved with gold, and its walls embedded with jewels. The river of life flows from the throne, and the tree of life yields healing fruit. The sights, sounds, and smells of God's habitation recorded in Revelation 21–22 stretch the limits of human imagination. Yet these are merely set dressing for the true pleasure of heaven: "Behold, the dwelling place of God is with man. He will dwell with them, and they will be his people, and God himself will be with them as their God" (Rev. 21:3). At the center of our pleasure in this paradise will be our pleasure in God himself.

So when we take a day each week to rest in anticipation of our final Sabbath rest, this is a day not of deprivation but of delight. This is a day not of fasting but of feasting. At the heart of Sabbath practice is enjoying God and his good gifts.

This means extending practices you should have every day. Spend an extra twenty minutes meditating on God's Word. Linger even longer as you commune with him through prayer. Find a park where you can take a long walk, either in adoring silence or with your worship playlist on repeat. If you practice Sabbath on Sunday, take time to prepare your heart for corporate worship, going in with a hunger and desire to find joy in God through singing, hearing his Word, and hearing from others about what they have experienced of God that week.

While this spiritual activity is core to our delight, remember that Jesus' return will bring about the renewal of the entire physical creation, that the "all things" God will make new include rivers and trees and bodies and food. So take time on your Sabbath to enjoy good things—read poetry, eat a delicious meal, listen to beautiful music, go hiking, laugh with family or friends. Break free of the cheap knockoffs of delight that our current day offers, whether ceaselessly scrolling through social media or numbing out in front of streaming shows. Practice pleasure in God and his good gifts, knowing that one day you will inhabit and enjoy his unspoiled, new creation forever.

Our Final, Forever Rest

My children grew accustomed to my dad's Sabbath practice. Before sundown on Friday nights, his alarm went off to remind him that it was time to prepare for his day of rest. When sundown came he gave a "Shabbat shalom!" to those in the house. My daughter Sophia particularly loved spending time with Grandpa during Sabbath, whether it was lighting special candles, reading God's Word together, or finding a dozen ways to have fun. She loved to "Shabbat shalom" with Grandpa, as she put it.

When we told Sophia that Grandpa had died, she immediately broke out into sobs of sorrow. She had a special heart connection with him. But later in the morning, once the initial wave of emotion died down, she realized it was Friday and tugged at Rachael's arm frantically: "Mama, Grandpa's going to miss Shabbat shalom!" To which Rachael replied, "No, honey, Grandpa is in Shabbat shalom now, and he will enjoy it forever."

Jesus is returning to make everything right. He will bring the final Sabbath of rest, of ceasing from labor to enjoy God and his good gifts. He will bring the final shalom—peace, wholeness, harmony, abundance. As we await the world Jesus will bring—no more pain, no more sorrow, no more death, no more decay—let's place all of our trust in him and commit a day each week to inhabit that world now.

Questions for Reflection

1. Do you take a weekly day of rest? If not, what are some of the barriers to regularly ceasing from labor?

2. Do you find it difficult to disconnect from productivity? If so, what do you think this says about your relationship with work?

3. What activities feel like play to you? How might you incorporate these into your weekly day of rest?

4. On our days of rest, we anticipate what Jesus will bring about at his return: the redemption of work, God's eternal rule, and eternal delight. Which of these do you need to nurture most on your next day of rest? How might you do that?

PART 4

THE TRANSFORMING POWER OF HOPE

In this final section we pivot to the application of all we have learned. How should our anticipation of Jesus' return change how we live today? How does this hope purify our hearts, transform our ministries to others, and fuel perseverance through afflictions?

If you are the practical sort, you may have flipped straight to this section to get to the "So what?" part of the book. Why bother with all of the explanations of Jesus' appearing when we can get down to brass tacks? While I could give a brief and bland answer, let me instead tell you about one of the worst summers in Davis family history.

In 2012, we experienced an arachnid attack. First it was the ticks. I am not talking about the handful of ticks that tried feasting on our dogs. I am talking about an invasion of ticks into our house. Since they are nearly uncrushable, we would drop them into the toilet. But by the time we were killing more than a hundred per day—as God is my witness—we tired of the bathroom trips and set up localized death pools in the form of old yogurt or sour-cream containers half filled with water.

Then it was the spiders. One Monday I was working in the yard when I was bitten three times by a black widow. By Tuesday afternoon I was delirious, and by Tuesday night the spot on my left ear and jaw where the bite happened turned into a puffy hive that marched, like Sherman to the sea, across my face from one ear to the other. Those three bites knocked me out for two weeks and compromised my health long after.

Needless to say, we did our research on how to reduce the arachnid presence in our home, and found one preeminent principle: control the environment. Wood piles and tall grass provide a welcome habitat for ticks and spiders. Wood piles and tall grass happened to be the exact environment I had allowed in our yard. It did not seem like a big deal at the time to mow but not trim, or to leave the wood on the ground, but now it mattered. Even the yard spray that is supposed to obliterate the arachnids had a warning to the effect of "if you are not going to cut down the tall grass in your yard, do not even bother to spray this stuff."

And that is the warning label I place on this final section. The environment of your spiritual life matters as much as individual decisions you make. Your struggle with that excessive drink of alcohol, that clever but devastating comment, that click on a pornographic image, that angry outburst does not happen in a vacuum. The discouragement you face in ministry is not isolated. The weariness you experience as you walk through afflictions has context. These take place within the spiritual environment you are cultivating.

So on the off chance that you skipped to this section in the spirit of "just tell me what to do," I hope you find the content here helpful. But please know that you cannot fight off the arachnids without cutting down the tall grass. Locating Jesus' return in the whole biblical story (chapters 1–3) and seeing a vision of Jesus' appearing (chapters 4–7) in the context of the rhythms we explored—gather, fast, rest (chapters 8–10)—are what will make the contents of this section sticky. What purifies you is not the willpower of one decision but a whole life that is shaped by Jesus' return.

CHAPTER 11

PURIFYING OURSELVES

This is the chapter that drove my study of Jesus' return long after the curiosity wore off. I needed to know how anticipating Jesus' return purifies all of the envy, pettiness, self-centeredness, lust, and greed out of my sinful heart. And the New Testament has a ton to say about that.

We're going to explore the promises, descriptions, and commands of the New Testament letters that show a direct connection between hope and purity of heart. It is a lot to digest. So to simplify all that we will see, let me direct your attention to the scene in John Bunyan's classic book *Pilgrim's Progress* where Christian and Faithful travel through the town called Vanity. In this town there is a year-round fair that offers everything the human heart could desire—land and houses, romance and sex, positions of power and the honor that comes with it, gold and all manner of fine jewelry. Vanity Fair also has ongoing entertainment—comedy, games, and hero stories. And if that gets boring, there are adulteries, murders, thefts, and betrayals to spice things up. It is a fair set up by the enemy himself to waylay those who are traveling toward the Celestial City.

The one thing that protects Christian and Faithful from buying what those merchants of sin are selling is their fixation on their destination. Their hope is set fully on the glory of the new Jerusalem, the Celestial City, and that attunement allows them to see the goods sold at Vanity Fair for what they are. And in the same way, it is fixing our hope on Christ and all that he will bring as Warrior King, Bridegroom, Judge, and Resurrecting One that empowers us to see the allurements of money, sex, power, comfort, and acclaim for the mirages that they are.

Today *Vanity Fair* is not a location but a glossy magazine you see at the grocery store checkout. Such is the insidious banality of modern temptation. Rather than being heralded by carnival barkers, it is wallpapered as the backdrop of our lives. You don't have to go to Sin City to feel the draw of "the lust of the flesh, the lust of the eyes, and the pride in one's possessions" (1 John 2:16 CSB). You only have to watch the commercials during the game.

I pray that as you walk through life barraged by the false promises of sin, in league with your own sin-bent inclinations, our overview of the New Testament's teaching points you to Jesus in such a way that empowers you to say yes to him and no to the passing pleasures of this age.

The Promises: He Will Hold Me Fast

When you look through the New Testament for texts that specifically connect our purity of life with the return of Jesus, you discover a beautiful dynamic. About half of the texts emphasize how we are supposed to live, and the other half contain promises that God will keep us to the end. While most of this chapter will work through the first category, I want to encourage you at the outset with the second. Your transformation from the sinful brokenness into which you were born to the moral beauty of Christ does not rest in your power. This is God's work. Paul promises that "[Jesus] will sustain you to the end, guiltless in the day" of his return (1 Cor. 1:7–8) and will bring the work he started in you to completion on that day (Phil. 1:6). As Jude writes, God "is able to keep you from stumbling and to present you blameless before the presence of his glory with great joy" (Jude 1:24).

This sampling of promises accompanies clear commands to walk in faithful obedience to Jesus. The apostles felt no need to delineate where God's power stops and our responsibility begins. Peter tells the church that they are being guarded for their final salvation both "by God's power" and "through faith" (1 Peter 1:5). Paul's instructions to the Thessalonians about love for one another follow his prayer, "May the Lord make you increase and abound in love for one another and for all . . . so that he may establish your hearts blameless in holiness before our God and Father, at the coming of our Lord Jesus with all his saints" (1 Thess. 3:12–13). Paul even feels this personally as he writes of "striving with [Christ's] strength that works powerfully in me" (Col. 1:29 CSB) and reports that his hard work in the gospel, harder than anyone else's, was "not I, but the grace of God that is with me" (1 Cor. 15:10).

Rather than dissecting this dynamic, let us acknowledge it and recognize the mystery that even our obedient response to God is fueled by him. As we roll up our sleeves to work, let us rest in the promise that God will supply the power necessary to walk in his ways. Be encouraged by Paul's holistic prayer and the promise of who will bring it about: "Now may the God of peace himself sanctify you completely, and may your whole spirit and soul and body be kept blameless at the coming of our Lord Jesus Christ. He who calls you is faithful; he will surely do it" (1 Thess. 5:23–24).

The Indicatives: What Sort of People Ought You to Be?

Among the texts that describe how we are supposed to live in light of Jesus' return, about half of those are descriptive. To use the verbal categories that all beginner Greek students learn, they are indicatives, not imperatives.

But by indicating what life shaped by Jesus' return should look like, the New Testament authors cause us to ask ourselves whether we truly believe what we say we believe. Consider Paul's words from Titus 2:12. By placing "ungodliness and worldly passions" next to "self-controlled, upright, and godly lives in the present age," Paul reminds us that all of our actions reveal something about our belief regarding the future. *Worldly* has taken on a life of its own in the church, often being applied to R-rated movies, alcohol, and books deemed spiritually dangerous. Calling these worldly misses the point. Something that is worldly is "of this world," bound to the values of this life, the assumptions of this present age.

So when I look at my own levels of self-control, just treatment of others ("upright"), and devotion to God ("godly"), I'm forced to ask, What do I truly believe? Do my actions reveal one who is trying to maximize his pleasure and comfort in this life, or am I living for the age to come? What do my sinful indulgences display about my actual beliefs? Do I hope in Jesus or in the things of earth?

Likewise, the indicatives of a life changed by Jesus' return challenge us to ask whether we believe enough in the glory of his appearing. John, after discussing our identity as children of God, shares a sense of wonderment that "what we will be has not yet appeared; but we know that when he appears we shall be like him, because we shall see him as he is. And everyone who thus hopes in him purifies himself as he is pure" (1 John 3:2–3).

According to John, the natural response to anticipating Jesus' return "as he is"—in his full resurrection splendor—is to purify ourselves, to hold an unmixed, unalloyed, singular desire to see Jesus face to face. So if I find myself fixating on how many Likes my social-media post garnered or cutting ethical corners to make more money, what does that reveal about how glorious I understand "as he is" to be? How much do I truly long to see Jesus if I'm bingeing reality TV shows to the neglect of making preparations?

The apostle Peter brings these indicative questions to a head. After painting an apocalyptic picture of the day of the Lord in which "the heavens will pass away with a roar, and the heavenly bodies will be burned up and dissolved, and the earth and the works that are done on it will be exposed," he asks this question: "What sort of people ought you to be in lives of holiness and godliness, waiting for and hastening the coming of the day of God!" (2 Peter 3:10–12).

Peter gives his own answer to this, as do Paul and John. Remember, these followers of Jesus had seen Jesus' blinding resurrection glory. They had fallen as though dead in his awesome presence. They never wanted it to end. So what sort of lives should we live as we wait for the ultimate "that Day"?

The Imperatives: Take Steps

As powerful as that self-reflection can be, when we move from these indicatives to the imperatives, we shift from how our lives ought to look to commands of things we should do in anticipation of Christ's return. We will explore five commands from the New Testament. They bring everything we've said thus far to a sharp point, calling us to a new kind of living that leans forward, to a life shaped by hope.

Hope Fully

Therefore, preparing your minds for action, and being sober-minded, set your hope fully on the grace that will be brought to you at the revelation of Jesus Christ.

—1 Peter 1:13

Take a moment to think about the next week, month, and year of your life. What are you hoping will happen? Whether it is a development in a relationship, a project at work, or a potential move, where does your anticipation lie?

I don't think Peter is commanding us to forsake any excitement about a new job or a dream vacation (or just making it to the weekend!). But for the follower of Jesus, these are lowercase *h* hopes that should pale in comparison with our capital *h* Hope. You can acknowledge your excitement about the upcoming visit with your close friend and the new restaurant you want to try while holding a real, sturdy, and if necessary, overriding hope in the revelation of Jesus.

There is a difference in our stride through life that such full hope creates. When I was in college, I worked as a resident assistant, which required a certain amount of hours each week in the central office for freshman housing. As I did homework or talked with friends, I could see the residents of the dorm walking through the lobby. Even in my peripheral vision, I could tell on the weekend evenings whether a resident was going to get a Coke from the machine (in the South every soda is a "Coke") or on their way to go swing dancing. How? By their stride. A trip to the Coke machine was a shuffle. A trip off campus for a big night was a long stride. Our hope affects our walk.

Peter's call to "hope fully" in the revealing of Jesus is clarified by the phrase "preparing your minds for action," which is literally translated "girding up the loins of your minds." (See Luke 12:35.) This was a posture of readiness in Peter's day—the long Middle Eastern robe tucked into the belt so that a person could move swiftly with long strides.

This invites us to evaluate how our small hopes relate to our great Hope. How do I walk? Am I striding toward the great hope of seeing Jesus face to face? Do I take long steps toward the love, justice, and joy that Jesus will bring? Or do I shuffle through life, easily influenced by the petty ambitions or anxieties of others, bogged down by pursuits that don't ultimately matter?

Stay Awake and Be Sober

> So then let us not sleep, as others do, but let us keep awake and be sober. For those who sleep, sleep at night, and those who get drunk, are drunk at night.
>
> —1 Thessalonians 5:6–7

In this passage about the day of the Lord, Paul employs two metaphors that need no explanation. Because Christ will come "like a thief in the night" (1 Thess. 5:2)—unexpectedly—the Thessalonians need to stay awake and be sober.

Paul identifies what will hinder such readiness: a mentality that says, "There is peace and security" (v. 3). Our home security system, financial savings, robust insurance policies, and extended warranties may make wise financial sense, but they can also give us a false sense of security. A person can have all the protections possible in this life and be unprepared for the day that will matter most.

As believers in Jesus, we should ask ourselves, What lulls

me to sleep? What intoxicates me? What dulls my spiritual senses and causes me to lose my readiness? What gives me a false sense of security?

The answer does not have to be something sinful. Often it is not. Good things such as a degree from a reputable school, respect in the community, and a loving family are gifts to be enjoyed. But they are not meant to cause us to settle into this life as if it is all there is. Likewise, sports and the arts and travel and restoring vintage cars and genealogical research and a thousand other interests are wonderful ways to enjoy God's world. But any good thing that becomes the center of our attention can make us spiritually drowsy or drunk. Such pursuits should make our short list of things to fast from, whether for an extended season or weekly, in anticipating Jesus' return.

Splash some water on your face and wake up! Paul commands, "Let us be sober, having put on the breastplate of faith and love, and for a helmet the hope of salvation" (v. 8). By centralizing the life of faith, not sight, and setting our hope on the final salvation Jesus will bring at his return, we can keep good gifts in their proper place and stay awake and sober.

Kill Sin

> When Christ who is your life appears, then you also will appear with him in glory. Put to death therefore what is earthly in you: sexual immorality, impurity, passion, evil desire, and covetousness, which is idolatry. On account of these the wrath of God is coming.
>
> —Colossians 3:4–6

Central to the work of purifying ourselves is ridding our lives of ongoing sinful behavior. But if you've been a Christian for more than two weeks, you know that there are some sins you can simply stop and others that seem to pull you back in with gravitational force. In this text Paul focuses on sexual sins and then moves on to sinful ways we use our speech: "anger, wrath, malice, slander, and obscene talk from your mouth. Do not lie to one another" (Col. 3:8–9).

Whatever makes your top list of "the sin that so easily entangles" (Heb. 12:1 NIV), Paul is not calling you to quit out of sheer willpower. Christ is the one who saves you from sin, not only by taking your punishment on the cross but also in giving you a new hope in his return.

Paul captures this in Colossians 3 with language of "above" and "on earth." Christ is above, "seated at the right hand of God" (v. 1). Because we who are one with Jesus by faith have been raised with him to that high place, Paul tells us to seek and "set your minds on things that are above, not on things that are on earth" (v. 2). There is the distinction. Your life is above with Christ, yet you are still living on earth. The call is to live an "above lifestyle" with an "above mentality" while on earth.

Think of the scene in the movie where the heroine looks at her small town and says, "There's nothing for me here. My future is in _____," whether that life ends up being in the big city, national politics, Hollywood, or med school. Her future shapes her decisions. And in the same way, Paul tells believers, "You have died, and your life is hidden with Christ in God" (v. 3). Our future, our destiny, our identity is all wrapped up with Christ above. It will all be revealed at his appearing when we are made glorious like him. (See chapter 7.)

Therefore, Paul argues, stop living in the ways of this tired world that is passing away. "You have died," so "put to death" what belongs to the old life (vv. 3, 5). Rather, since you have put on a new self, walk in new ways of kindness, humility, and patience. "Above all these put on love" (vv. 10, 12–17). In Christ this is who you are. It is who you will always be once he returns and you are glorified. Focus on Christ and his ways until sexual lust, anger, and lying seem backward and obsolete. Then leave those ways behind as you walk in Christ's love.

Be Diligent

> But the day of the Lord will come like a thief, and then the heavens will pass away with a roar, and the heavenly bodies will be burned up and dissolved, and the earth and the works that are done on it will be exposed. . . . Therefore, beloved, since you are waiting for these, be diligent to be found by him without spot or blemish, and at peace.
>
> —2 Peter 3:10, 14

Reading Peter's account of the day of the Lord—roaring heavens, dissolving planets—can feel like watching the climax of a superhero movie. You wonder, "What am I supposed to do with all of this destruction if I don't have a superpower?"

As it turns out, Peter has an answer for us. Since "the

earth and the works that are done on it will be exposed" (2 Peter 3:10), we are to be diligent about what spiritual state we are in when he finds us.

You might think that your moral purity would get lost in the shuffle with all the burning skies and melting elements. But that is what God is most interested in: What will be exposed in you when the earth is exposed? In what state will he find you?

This is not a scare tactic to cause you to question whether you will pass some final test. If you trust in Christ now, you will be saved from this destruction and God's wrath on that final day. But recall that when we looked at Jesus' return as Judge, we learned from Paul that a true love for Christ creates a desire to please him.

Peter invites us into this apocalyptic vision for the purpose of enhancing our spiritual diligence "to be found by him without spot or blemish, and at peace." Think of what might bring us spot or blemish, the things that might fracture our peace with God and one another. Is it resentment? Envy over a possession? Sexual lust? Hoarding of wealth? Now imagine that object of your desire—whether physical or symbolic—in the roaring fire of that final day. Where is the idol now? Did it endure the flames? Is it truly worthy of your attention and resources and longings?

The scorched-earth vision simplifies what matters in the same way that death does. I have officiated dozens of funerals, and families nearly always boil down what mattered most about the deceased to two things: faith and family. The money, the hobby, the possessions fade into the background.

What matters most is being right with God and at peace with one another. Let us be diligent to be found by him in this state.

Abide in Him

> And now, little children, abide in him, so that when he appears we may have confidence and not shrink from him in shame at his coming.
>
> —1 John 2:28

Our hope is not in an event but in a person—Jesus Christ. Our hope is not in the spectacle of his return but in remaining in his presence forever. Just as the greatest part of my wedding day was not the pageantry of the ceremony but the moment when we didn't part ways at the end of the night, what we long for most in Jesus' appearing is not the fireworks but the forever abiding, staying with him world without end.

The simplest way to prepare for the return of Christ is to abide in him now. *Abide* is one of John's favorite words to describe the intimate nature of being in relationship with Jesus. In his gospel he recorded Jesus' command, "Abide in me . . . my words abide in you . . . abide in my love . . . that my joy may be in you, and that your joy may be full" (John 15:1–11). It is such evocative, powerful language about our spiritual union with Jesus. In the physical realm, you cannot get closer than a branch that is grafted into a vine so that the vine's life-giving sap can flow through the branch and produce fruit. And in the spiritual realm, you cannot get closer than hearing and believing Jesus' words and making your needs known to him through prayer. This takes the form of daily Bible reading and meditation, journaling through the issues deep in your heart, silently receiving Jesus' love for you, worshiping Jesus through prayers of adoration or through song, and praying a simple affirmation, "Jesus, you are all I need."

Jesus' return will purify your heart when your expectation boils down to one thing: abiding in him. When dwelling in his presence is your supreme desire, then you can have confidence, when he returns, that you have spent your life on what matters most.

Questions for Reflection

1. Scan over the promises on pages 166–68. How does this assurance that God will sustain you to the end impact you?

2. What is one area of your life where your sinful actions force you to ask, "What do I truly believe?" Write out what you do believe and how you pray your actions will align with that belief.

3. What lulls you to sleep spiritually and dulls your spiritual senses? (These could be good or sinful things.) How can you fast periodically from these things to heighten your anticipation of Jesus' return?

4. What are the greatest distractions that keep you from abiding in Christ? What steps can you take to prioritize allowing his words, his love, and his joy to abide in you?

CHAPTER 12

DOING THE
MASTER'S WORK

W hen a man knows he is to be hanged in a fortnight, it concentrates his mind wonderfully."

What if Samuel Johnson's observation could apply to much more than the grim prospect of hanging and for much longer than two weeks? What if there were a looming event so weighty that it gives us laser focus for years?

For the apostle Paul, anticipating the coming of Jesus— that moment he would see his Savior face to face—wonderfully concentrated his mind for decades. Nowhere is this impact more pronounced than in his work of making disciples of Jesus Christ.

We are going to pivot from our previous focus on our own Christian life to explore how a full hope in Jesus' return can shape our ministry to others. To personalize the connection, think of three people whom God has put in your life for you to lead into deeper trust in and faithfulness to Christ— perhaps your children or grandchildren, neighbors, younger believers at church, or those who have sought you out to learn how to follow Jesus. Our goal in this chapter is to learn from Paul how anticipating Jesus' return can concentrate your mind wonderfully on your investment in these lives. We are going to join Paul in anticipating a particular moment that seemed to propel his ministry forward despite potential distractions and discouragements.

Paul faced the same challenges you might face with the three people you have in mind—spiritual and emotional immaturity (in ourselves or those we hope to disciple), difficulty finding time to meet together, physical illness, relational complications because of gossip from a third party.

Despite these distractions, Paul relentlessly forged ahead, preaching Christ where he was not yet known and calling those who believed to follow him into deeper, holistic faithfulness to Jesus. The fuel driving this ministry, what concentrated his mind so wonderfully, was his anticipation of the moment when he would present these disciples before Jesus, the risen Lord who had commissioned him for this work.

We're going to envision this moment and how it empowered Paul to carry out Jesus' commission to all believers: "make disciples of all nations" (Matt. 28:19). We need to see what Paul saw. Our shortsightedness that makes us want to tap out—focusing only on the slow growth of those we serve or our own immaturity that is unveiled by the relationship—needs to be supplemented by the long view. We don't need thicker skin; we need a longer stride as we move toward the moment when we will see Jesus and present to him those with whom we've shared his good news.

The Moment

Paul describes this moment in letters to three churches, suggesting that this was no passing thought but a driving vision behind his ministry. The most fully developed expression is in 1 Thessalonians 2:19–20. After being driven away from Thessalonica ("torn away from you . . . in person not in heart" [1 Thess. 2:17]) and then hearing about antagonists who questioned his motives, Paul wrote to assure the new church of his love and "great desire to see you face to face" (v. 17).

Despite the hindrances of both demonic and human opponents, Paul was intent on seeing his spiritual children again. This may be the most time-sensitive of Paul's letters, possibly written only weeks after he was driven away from Thessalonica and prevented from returning. Yet despite the immediacy of the situation, Paul's view remained fixed on the end: "For what is our hope or joy or crown of boasting before our Lord Jesus at his coming? Is it not you? For you are our glory and joy" (vv. 19–20).

Why was Paul so relentless in his ministry to the Thessalonians? Why was he willing to send Timothy back to follow up on them (3:1–10)? Why did Paul continue to instruct them about sexual holiness and brotherly love? Because one day Paul would stand before Jesus and present to him the Thessalonian believers.

This is the moment that concentrated Paul's mind wonderfully. It was all clear to him. He saw Jesus and he saw the Thessalonians who believed in Jesus through Paul's preaching. That was enough to drive Paul forward. Jesus was his crucified

Savior, his resurrected Lord, his returning Master. In response to Jesus' Damascus road call "to carry my name before the Gentiles and kings and the children of Israel" (Acts 9:15), Paul had carried it to Thessalonica. And Paul was eager to report back and show Jesus the people who now trusted in him through Paul's witness.

Though this moment is simple, it contains many layers. We're going to peel back three of those layers, one at a time, using this description: *In the moment when we see Jesus at his coming, we will boast in the faith of those with whom we shared the gospel and our selves.* After examining each layer, we will look at this moment as a whole to ask how it can fuel your spiritual investment in the three people you have identified.

Layer 1: Boasting

The other two times that Paul envisions this moment of seeing both Master and disciples share a surprising theme with the words in Thessalonians: boasting. Paul anticipates with the Corinthians that "on the day of our Lord Jesus you will boast of us as we will boast of you" (2 Cor. 1:14). And he calls the Philippians to a life made blameless and brilliant by the gospel, "so that in the day of Christ I may be proud that I did not run in vain or labor in vain" (Phil. 2:16).

In all three texts, Paul's "boast" or being "proud" or "crown of boasting" translates the word *kauchēma*. It is a word Paul uses to describe sinful boasting (Rom. 3:27; 1 Cor. 5:6;

Gal. 6:14; Eph. 2:9) as well as godly boasting (1 Cor. 9:15–16; 2 Cor. 5:12; 7:4; 8:24; 9:3; 11:10). The latter carries all of the exultation and pride of sinful boasting with none of the corrupted self-focus. This may be difficult for us to imagine, since our smallest and simplest acts can be infiltrated by self-exaltation. But if you have ever seen the moment when a new mother shows her parents their grandchild for the first time, you know that guileless, grateful joy that characterizes the good kind of *kauchēma*.

Such was Paul's boasting in these churches. Like a proud papa, he bragged about his spiritual children to others and anticipated the day when he would boast in them before Jesus himself at his return.

This moment of boasting before Jesus concentrated his mind wonderfully by relativizing both his accomplishments and his suffering. Shortly before calling the Philippians (like he had the Thessalonians) "my joy and crown" with whom he awaits "a Savior, the Lord Jesus Christ," Paul compared his impressive rabbinical resume to a dung heap and joyfully embraced suffering, even to death, all for the sake of knowing and gaining Christ (Phil. 3:7–4:1). He had relocated his sense of success from his past high standing among other Pharisees to that future moment of seeing Christ and parading the followers of Jesus before him.

Think about the things people normally boast about: fitness goals, academic degrees, military rank, financial security, a network of influencers, recognition in your field, a product you have created, the academic or athletic achievements of your children, or whatever else lies before you as a mile marker of success. These are the types of things we boast in, whether we do it out loud or internally when we mentally compare our accomplishments with those of others.

But what if our posture toward boasting were revolutionized? Without downplaying the fruit of our labor or the importance of hard work, what if we, like Paul, shifted our hope fully from the items on our resume now to the moment of Jesus' return? What if our boast was not the master's degree but the people we invested in spiritually while pursuing it, not the promotion at work but the way we modeled Christlikeness to new subordinates, not the honors program our child got into but the way we trained her to steward her gifts for the glory of God and the good of others?

One of my mentors always told me, "Ministry is people." And what will matter when we stand before Christ are the people whom we pointed to Christ.

Layer 2: Faith

So what is it about these folks we minister to that we will boast in?

Let's go back to Paul's situation with the Thessalonians. He has been involuntarily removed from them, knows they've been fed lies about his intentions, and urgently sends Timothy to check on them. What is Timothy supposed to assess?

The answer is unmistakable and gives more focus to what we will boast in before Jesus: faith.

"We sent Timothy, our brother and God's coworker in

the gospel of Christ, to establish and exhort you in your *faith*" (1 Thess. 3:2, emphasis added).

And again, "For this reason, when I could bear it no longer, I sent to learn about your *faith*, for fear that somehow the tempter had tempted you and our labor would be in vain" (v. 5, emphasis added).

And Timothy's report back? "But now that Timothy has come to us from you, and has brought us the good news of your *faith* . . . we have been comforted about you through your *faith*. For now we live, if you are *standing fast in the Lord*" (vv. 6–8, emphasis added).

As Paul imagines standing before Jesus at his coming and boasting in the Thessalonians, what he will boast in is their faith, their trust in Jesus. He echoes a similar sentiment when he tells the Philippians that his hope in being found not guilty and released from prison is that "I will remain and continue with you all, for your progress and joy in the faith" (Phil. 1:25). Seeing Jesus would be better, should he be executed, but he is eager to work with them that their "boasting in Christ Jesus may abound" (v. 26 CSB).

This brings tremendous clarity to what matters most as we engage others. When you stand before Jesus in his unveiled glory, what you will boast about is how you helped these fellow disciples trust Jesus more. All that time you spent studying the Bible together was meant to bolster their faith. All those hours you invested showing why the promises of God are worth trusting over the allurements of money, sex, and power were meant to build up faith. All the compassionate listening you did to stories of abuse and neglect was done in the hope that they would see in you a model of divine care and have faith again in the Father's love.

Our highest concern in the lives of those we invest in is their faith. We cannot make anyone do anything, but we can challenge them toward a growing, deepening trust in Jesus from which obedience flows. And Paul's model allows us to peel back one more layer to ask how we go about nurturing the faith of others.

Layer 3: Sharing

Because Paul recounts his recent time with the Thessalonians, we get to observe a master class in gospel ministry. The heart of it is found in 1 Thessalonians 2:8: "So, being affectionately desirous of you, we were ready to share with you not only the gospel of God but also our own selves, because you had become very dear to us."

In the surrounding verses, Paul connects concrete actions with this beautiful sentiment. He reminds them of the numerous times he had proclaimed the gospel of God to the Thessalonians, despite pushback and the unpopularity of the message. Likewise, he fleshes out what it means for his ministry team to share "our own selves" (v. 8): "We worked night and day"—most likely making and selling tents, as that was Paul's trade—"that we might not be a [financial] burden to any of you" (v. 9). They kept their conduct blameless, not chasing after the Thessalonians' praise or their purses. And their spiritual parenting reflected both paternal instruction (vv. 11–12) and maternal nurture (vv. 5–7).

This is a robust vision of what kind of ministry develops the faith of others. Under the heading of sharing the gospel and ourselves falls everything from Bible study to empathetic listening to financial sacrifice to checking our motives for being involved in people's lives in the first place.

And it is this personal, life-on-life nature of gospel ministry that can lead to frustration. We pour ourselves out for others, making every effort to model Christlikeness, show patience, confront sin, give correction, resolve conflict, and instruct with God's Word, whether or not it is socially acceptable. At times we minister to Philippians or Thessalonians, where there is joyful, appreciative growth. And at times we minister to Corinthians, where there is pettiness, arrogance, and questioning of our motives.

In such times we need to zoom out through the layers we just pulled back. The reason we are sharing the gospel and ourselves with others is because we want to nurture their faith in Jesus. We want to nurture their faith in Jesus because we will boast in them before Jesus when he returns. And doing so will bring us joy because Jesus is everything to us and our hearts' desire is to please him.

Such a long view can concentrate our minds wonderfully. That vision of boasting to Jesus in the faith of those we serve can help us see beyond the immediate frustrations of ministry to the final day of exuberantly saying, "Jesus, I did what you told me to do!"

Basking in the Moment

In the moment when we see Jesus at his coming, we will boast in the faith of those with whom we shared the gospel and our selves. Let yourself behold that scene, populating it with the three people you identified earlier, those with whom you share the gospel and yourself. Name them. See the backs of their heads as you stand among them. Take in the memories of long conversations, excited progress, frustrating conflict, and spiritual breakthroughs.

Now lift your eyes to Jesus. See his brilliant, authoritative, ever-living majesty. Hear the sound of his voice like the roar of many waters. Tremble at his holy, fiery judgment. Taste the relief of his merciful sacrifice to rescue you from that judgment. Behold in him the Lion of Judah and the Lamb of God.

Now. What matters most in that moment?

The answer is, of course, Jesus. I see a host of redeemed sinners pointing at the risen Christ with looks on their faces of joy and reverence and wonder and exhilaration, simply shouting "You!" This is worship, our eternal vocation. And now imagine the smile on your face widening as you look around at those standing with you and add, "I helped them trust in you!"

That will be something to boast about. It won't have anything to do with you. It's all about Jesus. And the crowd of those you helped will increase your joy on that final day. Of all the crowns and jewels and robes in that heavenly experience, nothing will be a greater reward than looking at the dozens, hundreds, even thousands with whom you shared the gospel and yourself and knowing that you poured yourself out that they might trust joyfully in the one who matters most.

Spirit and Scope

Let's return from that sublime moment to your life today, noting two dynamics in your ministry. The first is the Holy Spirit. We have isolated moments when Paul anticipates boasting in the faith of the Philippian, Corinthian, and Thessalonian believers. We would be negligent to leave out the indispensable activity of the Holy Spirit in this work. Yes, Paul preached the gospel to the Thessalonians. But he saw evidence of God's saving power because his gospel was delivered "also in power and in the Holy Spirit and with full conviction" (1 Thess. 1:5). As Paul summarizes his ministry to the Romans, in anticipation of their supporting his gospel work, he boldly says, "I have reason to be proud of my work for God" (Rom. 15:17). Then he clarifies that boasting: "For I will not venture to speak of anything except what Christ has accomplished through me to bring the Gentiles to obedience—by word and deed, by the power of signs and wonders, by the power of the Spirit of God" (vv. 18–19).

We must never forget that the only *spirit*ual growth that happens in the lives of others is the work the Spirit does. Like Elijah, we can set up the sacrifice on the altar, but God has to bring the fire. Like Paul, we can plant, and like Apollos, we can water, but God must give the growth. This necessarily sends us to our knees, resting in the Lord's final work to bring about faith in those we serve.

The second dynamic is the question of scope. Paul's explanation of his ministry in Romans 15 continues: "So that from Jerusalem and all the way around to Illyricum I have fulfilled the ministry of the gospel of Christ; and thus I make it my ambition to preach the gospel, not where Christ has already been named, lest I build on someone else's foundation" (vv. 19–20).

Paul was drawing a map for the Roman Christians, showing them the scope of his apostolic ministry, in the hope that they would support his mission to take the gospel to Spain (v. 24). Regarding the places where he had already planted churches, he said, "I no longer have any room for work in these regions" (v. 23). This doesn't mean that there were no more unbelievers left or that the believers were mature. It means only that Paul has finished his specific task of pioneer mission work and church planting where formerly Christ was not named.

At the same time, Paul's scope was distinct from that of Peter, John, Timothy, Titus, and a host of other gospel ministers. I identify this distinction to invite you into prayerful consideration of the scope of the ministry God has given you. It may be narrow and deep, like raising small children or working with those traumatized by abuse or neglect. It may be broad and brief, like helping business owners bring a chaplain into their workplace. It may be local to the town where you grew up, speaking the good news of Jesus in the language and customs of your people. It may be global, as God calls you to your "Spain" of an unreached people group in India, Saudi Arabia, or Indonesia.

God's Spirit may use you to nurture deep faith in a few, the beginnings of faith in many, or something in between.

Whatever the scope of the work, may the Spirit empower and propel you as you anticipate the moment when you will see Jesus at his coming and boast in the faith of those with whom you shared the gospel and yourself.

Questions for Reflection

1. How would you describe the scope of the ministry God has called you to?

2. Write out the names of the three people you identified whom God has called you to invest in spiritually.

3. Walk through the mental exercise on pages 188–89. Describe what you see and how you feel.

4. How might this vision motivate you to focus on nurturing the faith of those you serve?

5. How might this vision motivate you to share the gospel more intentionally and yourself more freely with them?

6. It is ultimately the Spirit's work to produce lasting fruit in people's lives. Write out a prayer for the three people you listed, asking God to grow faith and love in their lives through your labor.

CHAPTER 13

PERSEVERING THROUGH AFFLICTIONS

Jesus did not relegate the possibility of afflictions in the Christian life to the fine print:

"FOLLOW ME!"

Warning: Side effects of following Jesus may include persecution, marginalization, divisions between parents and children, being driven from your hometown, imprisonment, torture, and death.

No, as off-putting as it may have been for public relations and recruiting, Jesus placed suffering and persecution in bold letters on the marquee. His call to discipleship was accompanied by references to losing your life and following him to execution. He told his disciples, "If they persecuted me, they will also persecute you" (John 15:20). After his resurrection, he told Peter he would be a martyr and sent the message to

Paul, "I will show him how much he must suffer for the sake of my name" (Acts 9:16).

The good news is that when Jesus invites us to follow him, he calls us to follow his entire journey through suffering into resurrection glory. So the same connection to Jesus that will lead us through persecution will yield a glorious end.

My burden in this book has been to fill out the robust nature of knowing and following Jesus, not only in his death and resurrection but also in his return. It is that very arc that not only explains why afflictions accompany Christian faithfulness but also gives us hope to persevere well through them.

The New Testament offers ample encouragement to endure suffering for Christ's sake. But it also addresses our broader experience of suffering and injustice in a fallen world, not necessarily tied to our Christian identity. Peter writes about "various trials" (1 Peter 1:6), and as we will see in James, "trials of various kinds" (James 1:2) include workplace injustice and class prejudice.

Whether or not the difficulty we face is a result of our faith in Jesus, the hope we hold in his appearing can carry us through such trials. To that hope we look now as we explore four ways in which Jesus' return empowers our perseverance through affliction.

1. Persevere with Prophetic Patience

"Be patient until the Lord's coming" (James 5:7 CSB). These words, written by Jesus' half brother, spoke to a particular kind of affliction in the early years of the church. This specificity may help us understand how anticipating Jesus' return informs our experiences of abuse and injustice today.

James's call to patience is directed toward field hands who harvested for powerful, wealthy landowners. The landowners held back the wages of these workers for no other reason than that they had the power to do so.

Our nation saw this dynamic in Southern states following America's civil war. Many formerly enslaved persons in the South became sharecroppers, often working the same land for their former masters. Because the landowners had all of the legal and social power, they often forced the black (and sometimes white) laborers into unjust contracts or simply withheld their wages. I heard an elderly African American man tell his story—representative of the time—of watching this injustice unfold. His father presented meticulously kept books of how much he owed the landowner for seed, fertilizer, and farming equipment, how much cotton he had grown for the man, how much cotton was selling for, and thus how much he had come out ahead. It was going to be a good year. They were going to be able to pocket a good bit of the profits, perhaps to buy some land of their own. But after the landowner looked over the father's accounting, he simply said, "No, according to my books we broke even this year. I don't owe you a thing."

The old man telling the story remembered the indignation he felt as a little boy. He started to say something, to protest, to demand justice, but his father squeezed his hand to silence him. The father stood there, stoic, knowing that a sharecropper's word would never be believed over a landowner's, knowing that a black man in the South could be lynched for stepping out of line, knowing that the white power structure would never give him his justice. So he just said "yes, sir" as the man robbed him of his wages.

This is the kind of situation James is addressing when he calls God's people to patience. He highlights dynamics of social power structures that might not change in his lifetime.

Yet James is not telling them to roll over and play dead, to become doormats. Rather, his call is to a prophetic patience. Prophetic patience submits to God's timeline of justice while crying out about that justice now.

James not only points to the prophets as examples— "As an example of suffering and patience, brothers, take the prophets who spoke in the name of the Lord" (James 5:10)— he himself models this prophetic stance toward the wealthy landowners. He calls them to "weep and howl for the miseries that are coming upon you" (James 5:1). He mocks their already decaying ill-gotten gain. He amplifies the voices of the victims of their injustice, assuring them that "the cries of the harvesters have reached the ears of the Lord of hosts" (v. 4). The oppressors may have lived fat and happy, but the fattening was for "a day of slaughter" (v. 5).

By speaking in this way, James acknowledges both that final justice will be brought about only at the coming of the Lord and that justice should be addressed now. "Behold," he tells them in verse 9, "the Judge is standing at the door." The return of Christ is the great hope that what is inequitable, exploitative, abusive, and harmful will be set right. And our daily prayer, meant to shape our engagement with this present state of affairs, is "your kingdom come, your will be done, on earth as it is in heaven" (Matt. 6:10).

James illustrates prophetic patience with the experience of the farmers he is addressing: "See how the farmer waits for the precious fruit of the earth, being patient about it, until it receives the early and the late rains. You also, be patient. Establish your hearts, for the coming of the Lord is at hand" (James 5:7–8).

The farmers James is referencing would plant their seed in the fall. And then there was absolutely nothing they could do to force that seed to grow. They simply had to wait until the early rains came around October and November, then the latter rains in March and April. Wait. Wait. Wait.

And so it is with the injustice they face. The fruit of justice will grow. Jesus will bring a harvest of equity when he comes. But those exploited laborers can't hurry it or force it into being any more than they can make a seed sprout. They have to establish their hearts and wait expectantly for his return.

But farming is not all waiting, is it? If you have been around a farm, you know that a farmer doesn't sit back and do nothing between planting season and harvest. The farmer is working from sunup to sundown—pulling weeds, keeping birds away from the seed, spreading manure, and tending to the animals that create the manure. So the farmer is both waiting and active.

Perhaps you are an abuse survivor whose painful story of betrayal and coverup burns deep in your heart. Perhaps you have been socially marginalized or financially disadvantaged because of your gender, ethnicity, or skin color. Perhaps your dedication to repairing a tear in the social fabric has brought unwarranted criticism from believers who hold different political views.

Whatever your experience of injustice or exclusion, there is a pathway of prophetic patience God invites you to walk. He calls you to cry out about what is wrong as you wait for the coming of the Lord. This is not a denial of the horrific things you have suffered. It is not resignation to the status quo under which you were harmed. Your persistent advocacy may bring about accountability for those misusing power and institutional change. But even if it does not, your hope can rest secure in the fact that the movie will have a good ending because the coming King Jesus will acknowledge your pain, vindicate your suffering, and set right what is wrong in this world.

2. Persevere without Grumbling

In the middle of his treatment of patience through suffering, James inserts a word that, on the first reading, feels like an unanticipated left turn. "Do not grumble against one another . . . so that you may not be judged; behold, the Judge is standing at the door" (James 5:9).

Why bring up grumbling in the context of affliction?

If you have been in a high-pressure situation before, you know how snippy people can get. I heard a podcaster say that his family refers to him as "Airport Brian" when they are on a trip, because in airports he becomes the most exasperated, panicked version of himself. Rachael and I laugh about it because it perfectly describes me. When our children were younger, we would fly from Phoenix to Charlotte to Atlanta. This was quite the operation, especially when our daughter was three and our twin boys were two. When a bag was too heavy and we were in two different security lines and one child had to go to the bathroom and another's sippy cup was leaking, I was not the model of patience and grace. I started barking and blaming, and suddenly vacation wasn't very fun.

James is speaking to people who are in the high-pressure situation of oppression and poverty. They are being robbed of their wages and have no recourse, and consequently their kids will go to bed hungry and they face losing everything they own. That's a tremendous weight to carry, and it can lead to grumbling—blaming this person, accusing that person, lashing out verbally, exerting what little power you can because most of your power has been stripped away.

But James reminds them that the same event they can't wait for—the coming of the Lord Jesus as Judge—means judgment for all sinners, not only rich sinners. So James warns them about being judged, since "the Judge is standing at the door." Being patient through afflictions means waiting for Jesus to come in judgment and being ready for that judgment ourselves. It means not only asking God to save me from the oppression I face but also asking God to save me from sinful responses to that oppression, like taking frustration out on those closest to me.

Any mention of grumbling in the Bible recalls the grumbling of the Hebrews as they sojourned through the wilderness from Egypt to the promised land. Time and time again their complaints exposed hearts that did not believe that Yahweh would fulfill his promises to bring them into the land. God's question to Moses, "How long shall this wicked congregation grumble against me?" (Num. 14:27) paralleled his earlier questions, "How long will this people despise me? And how long will they not believe in me, in spite of all the signs that I have done among them?" (v. 11).

These cries of "How long?" regarding unbelief stand in stark contrast with the "How long?" found in psalms of lament like Psalms 6, 13, 35, 79, 89, and 94. In those contexts, the psalmist cries out to God, believing that he will show *hesed*, covenant faithfulness, but not knowing when he will make good on his promises. It is the cry of covenantal complaining, a longing for the fulfillment of God's word with the assumption that it will happen.

When we find ourselves grumbling against one another in times of high pressure, this is an invitation to evaluate whether we truly trust God to execute justice and vindicate his people. If so, how might we look to other believers as those who can help shore up our faith rather than as people to blame for our troubles? How might psalms of lament better vocalize the aching of our hearts? How can we welcome others into our groanings to both acknowledge our frustrations and remind us of God's faithfulness?

3. Persevere with Joy

The opposite response of grumbling and blaming is joy. James opens his letter by calling the church to "count it all joy . . .

when you meet trials of various kinds" (James 1:2). This springs from Jesus' stunning teaching in the Sermon on the Mount to "rejoice and be glad" when "others revile you and persecute you and utter all kinds of evil against you falsely on my account" (Matt. 5:11–12).

The New Testament is filled with such teaching, but the text that most clearly connects joy in afflictions with Jesus' coming was written by Peter. Before we hear his words, let's pause to appreciate Peter's relationship to suffering. This is the disciple who rebuked Jesus when he told the Twelve that he would be crucified. This is the disciple who pulled out his sword and started swinging when the soldiers came to arrest Jesus in the garden. Peter is the disciple who boldly proclaimed that he would never deny Jesus, only to do so three times when the chips were down. Peter's track record of suffering for Jesus was not stellar in the Gospels.

This is what makes Jesus and Peter's postresurrection interaction so poignant. After restoring Peter by asking him three times, "Do you love me?" Jesus told Peter what kind of end he would face. "When you were young, you used to dress yourself and walk wherever you wanted, but when you are old, you will stretch out your hands, and another will dress you and carry you where you do not want to go" (John 21:18). In case the florid language is lost on us, the author inserts this clarification: "This he said to show by what kind of death he was to glorify God" (v. 19). Then Jesus spoke his final words to Peter, echoing his words at their first encounter: "Follow me."

When you read Peter's first letter, it sounds like the implications of "Follow me" have finally sunk in. This was not "follow me to kick Rome out of Israel" or "follow me to rule the nation right now" but "follow me in my trajectory of suffering and glory." Here is what Peter wrote: "Beloved, do not be surprised at the fiery trial when it comes upon you to test you, as though something strange were happening to you. But rejoice insofar as you share Christ's sufferings, that you may also rejoice and be glad when his glory is revealed. If you are insulted for the name of Christ, you are blessed, because the Spirit of glory and of God rests upon you" (1 Peter 4:12–14).

The joy, Peter argues, is because of Christ. Peter had heard this before when Jesus told his disciples to rejoice and be glad when they were persecuted "on my account." To the degree that they found joy in Christ, they would find joy in suffering for Christ and with Christ. (See Paul's version of this idea in Phil. 3:7–11.) Finally, Peter understood that the focus of Jesus' "Follow me" was the "me." Jesus is our reward, our pearl of great price, our light, our salvation, our hope. To have Christ is to have everything, so to suffer with him is a privilege.

Peter taught these words out of experience. Following Pentecost, when his Spirit-anointed preaching rocked Jerusalem, Peter and John were brought before the Sanhedrin multiple times and commanded to cease from preaching in Jesus' name. The second time, the Sanhedrin had them beaten. At this, Peter and John "left the presence of the council, rejoicing that they were counted worthy to suffer dishonor for the name" (Acts 5:40–41).

The key to experiencing joy in afflictions is experiencing

joy in Christ. As Peter wrote at the beginning of his letter (and we surveyed in chapter 1), "Though you have not seen him, you love him. Though you do not now see him, you believe in him and rejoice with joy that is inexpressible and filled with glory" (1 Peter 1:8). Love and glorious joy in the crucified, risen, and returning Christ will see us through afflictions for Christ's sake with joy.

If you are facing a particularly difficult season of suffering, you may want to spend extended time reading the Gospels and meditating on Jesus' sufferings. Pause over what he endured, how he responded, and the way he found refuge in the presence of his Father. See yourself there with Jesus and ask the Spirit to grant you to truly know Christ as you "share his sufferings" (Phil. 3:10). As you share in Jesus' sufferings now and taste joy in his presence, you can be sure, to quote Peter again, that you will "rejoice and be glad when his glory is revealed" (1 Peter 4:13).

Because of our nation's painful history of enslavement and oppression, it is worth clarifying that the call to rejoice through afflictions is to be applied by the one facing the affliction, not suggested by the one causing it. Teachings like these were tragically deployed by antebellum preachers and enslavers to justify the suffering they were inflicting. As we consider this in our day, we must look at the afflictions others endure as opportunities to be a prophetic voice. How might we simultaneously encourage brothers and sisters to taste joy through suffering and ask how we might play a role in alleviating this suffering? The practice of joy and the pursuit of justice should go hand in hand as we seek to live faithfully under our King.

4. The Call to Conquer

We have largely avoided the book of Revelation in our study, since the symbolic nature of that great book has yielded a variety of end-times interpretations throughout church history. But in the early, least ambiguous chapters of Revelation, there is one word that brings powerful clarity to what it looks like to persevere through afflictions in view of Christ's return.

In each of the seven letters Jesus writes to congregations in western Turkey, he holds out a promise "to the one who conquers." That's the word: conquer.

On the surface, *conquer* has a triumphal, aggressive, even violent connotation, evoking images of crusaders and conquistadors. The true meaning is quite the opposite. According to Robert Mounce, "The overcomers in Revelation are not those who have conquered an earthly foe by force, but those who have remained faithful to Christ to the very end. The victory they achieve is analogous to the victory of Christ on the cross."[41]

There was a time when I thought that "remaining faithful to the end" was a lame life goal. Then I saw one friend after another, one hero after another, fall prey to this or that temptation. Now this definition of conquering feels much more noble.

In the seven letters to the churches in Asia, Jesus identifies the challenges to conquering: false teaching, indulgence in the idolatry and sexual immorality of the culture, spiritual apathy, financial hardship, and persecution. These were typically intertwined, because the persecution and poverty often arose from the church's refusal to participate in the idolatrous, immoral festivities of the trade guilds. Politics, religion, and economics were inextricably bound in these gatherings, and the church's absence from parties in honor of patron gods brought great consequences.

Jesus doesn't call these churches to conquer by transforming the Roman Empire or reforming the trade guilds. He calls them to "hold fast what you have until I come" (Rev. 2:25). Jesus would bring the judgment. They simply needed to hold on to him and bear witness to his love in word and deed.

None of this should lead us to a disengaged, hermetic existence, holed up in a cave waiting for Jesus' return. The church's faithfulness eventually did bring change to the Roman Empire and, more important, outlasted it. But the call to conquer does release us from feeling the burden of changing the world. We leave that to Jesus and focus on faithfulness to him and love for neighbor. Indeed, the great challenge of the Christian life is to engage our world without being spiritually deformed by its values. As we announce the news of Christ's conquering work—his death, resurrection, and promised return—we conquer by laying down our lives for others as he did for us. Ours too can be the testimony that "they have conquered [Satan] by the blood of the Lamb and by the word of their testimony, for they loved not their lives even unto death" (Rev. 12:11).

With Joy

In his letter to the Colossians, Paul prays that the church will be "strengthened with all power, according to his glorious might, for all endurance and patience with joy" (Col. 1:11). If you are in a challenging season right now, you know what a tall order endurance and patience are in the midst of afflictions. But joy? It feels humanly impossible.

Unless the whole thing is real. If Jesus really is returning as Warrior King, Bridegroom, Judge, and Resurrecting One, then you can put one foot in front of the other with joy, looking beyond "the sufferings of this present time" to "the glory that is to be revealed" (Rom. 8:18). He is greater than all the forces arrayed against you. His love and beauty will shine long after the afflictions that overwhelm you now are forgotten. May you love his appearing, striding toward that day with full hope.

Questions for Reflection

1. In what situations have you been on the receiving end of injustice with little power to change what is wrong? How might James's call to prophetic patience sustain you through those kinds of afflictions?

2. Whether or not you are suffering afflictions now, how can you lend a prophetic voice to injustice you see in your context?

3. Where are you tempted to direct your grumbling when you face affliction? What do you think grumbling reveals about your heart in that moment? How could focusing on Jesus' return as Judge address your temptation to grumble?

4. The key to experiencing joy in afflictions is experiencing joy in Jesus. Yet afflictions can overwhelm us such that we forget to prioritize our time spent with Jesus. How can you create more space in your day for Scripture meditation, prayer, listening to worship music, or spending time with spiritual mentors?

EPILOGUE

Over lunch with Steve and Celestia Tracy, mentors of Rachael's and mine, I shared the idea of a book that focused on how the return of Christ should transform our daily lives. Steve loved the idea, but his reason surprised me. "We don't think about death nearly enough in the American church. A renewed focus on Jesus' coming allows us to think about our personal end of life honestly, with hope rather than despair."

Steve shared this years before I wrote *Bright Hope for Tomorrow*, and his words ring even more true now. I write this as the COVID-19 virus brings on a surge of new deaths. I write this on the day I learned that my spiritual mentor from middle and high school finally succumbed to the deteriorating effects of Parkinson's disease. As you read this, you are absorbing personal news and national or international news about death and decay, betrayal and brokenness, a world falling apart. In such a state there is a temptation toward despair.

Or perhaps things are on the uptick for you. You got the promotion, started a new and exciting project, or just welcomed a child or grandchild into the world. There is enough beauty and goodness in your immediate view that you aren't much concerned with hope. In such a time there is a temptation toward ignoring the inevitable.

Wherever you are, what pushes you through those temptations and grounds you today in the reality not only of *your* end but *the* end is the bright hope that the Christ who died, the Christ who is risen is the Christ who will come again. Only by reckoning with that end can you honestly, meaningfully be present with your joys and challenges now.

There is one text I have not yet treated in this book, largely because it is a primary text that has been used to make a case for a secret rapture that precedes and is separated from Christ's second coming. Because it could raise debates about views of the tribulation and millennium, I have focused on the abundance of texts that more plainly address the way Christ's return should transform how we live.

But 1 Thessalonians 4:13–18 is too precious to leave to the side out of concern over controversy. Whatever your view of the end times may be, let me share how these verses speak into the life of the church I pastor.

At every funeral I officiate, I read verses 13–14 at the opening of the service: "We do not want you to be uninformed, brothers and sisters, concerning those who are asleep, so that you will not grieve like the rest, who have no hope. For if we believe that Jesus died and rose again, in the same way, through Jesus, God will bring with him those who have fallen asleep" (CSB).

At this point I usually direct our attention to the casket or urn. We ponder this particular death. Together we grieve, not as if this is the end for this person but feeling the aching absence of their presence now. And we hope. We fully hope that for the one who believes that Jesus died and rose again, this is only the beginning.

Paul grounds his hope on what we expect on that day: "For we say this to you by a word from the Lord: We who are still alive at the Lord's coming will certainly not precede those who have fallen asleep. For the Lord himself will descend from heaven with a shout, with the archangel's voice, and with the trumpet of God, and the dead in Christ will rise first. Then we who are still alive, who are left, will be caught up together with them in the clouds to meet the Lord in the air, and so we will always be with the Lord. Therefore encourage one another with these words" (1 Thess. 4:15–18 CSB).

Over the dull roar of social media Likes and ceaseless cable news and weeping for the tragic and laughing at the inane, Jesus will *shout*. The shout will be so loud and authoritative that the dead will hear it. As previewed in the raising of Lazarus (John 11:43) and the little girl (Mark 5:41), "an hour is coming, and is now here, when the dead will hear the voice of the Son of God, and those who hear will live" (John 5:25).

This is an epic moment great enough to capture your imagination and carry you in hope for the duration of your days. It will have all the fanfare of Mount Sinai in Exodus 19, with loud voice and trumpet blast.[42] It will carry all the trembling and awe of the divine manifestation when the people wondered whether they would make it out of the encounter alive. It will be a moment of transcendent joy for the dead and the living—if you are in Christ, you will be with Christ in person, day 1 of eternal communion.

The hope toward which we lean, the hope that transforms your day today is centered on the simple promise "and so we will always be with the Lord." Jesus is our hope, his presence our reward. By the Spirit we taste this hope now. On that final day we will luxuriate in his presence forever.

Paul's final words in verse 18 reinforce the thesis of this book, that the return of Christ is not meant to be a doctrine we debate or the center of a complex end-times system that stirs disagreement. What *are* Paul's words for? He writes to this persecuted young church, "Therefore encourage one another with these words."

I can do no better as I close this book. As you reorient your life around the day of Christ's return, encourage one another with these words. In the immediate context, the encouragement is for those who mourn the death of brothers and sisters in Christ. Encourage them to grieve with hope, joining in their sorrow that a loved one is no longer present with them, yet holding firm to the hope that they will together be with Christ forever.

"Encourage one another with these words" expands beyond a funeral context into the nooks and crannies of normal Tuesday mornings and exhausted Thursday nights and leisurely Saturday afternoons. Encourage one another in the places where you might least expect the reality of Christ's return to shape life:

- Encourage the mother of three young children, drowning in diapers and balancing nap schedules, that the developmental markers in which she hopes—sleeping through the night, potty training, the first day of school—are but practice runs for the final day that will give all of our relational investment meaning and reward.

- Encourage the nursing-home resident who counts his remaining life in months rather than years that he can finish the race well as one who, like Paul, loves Jesus' appearing. Invite him to meditate on the robust images of the Lord's coming in God's Word and to share this hope with the staff and other residents.

- Encourage the young woman in your church on her meteoric rise through the company ranks to steward her relationships in the workplace with a view of seeing Christ one day and joyfully showing him the colleagues who trust in him because of her work and witness.

- Encourage the family pulled this way and that by school events, sports, and music lessons to prioritize rhythms of gathering, fasting, and resting so that trust and hope in Jesus Christ can have the highest importance in their family life.

Friends, Jesus is coming! Encourage one another with these words.

ACKNOWLEDGMENTS

It is a surreal privilege to acknowledge those whose encouragement and help have led to the publication of this book. Though the list of names is too long for this space, I feel profound gratitude and hope you will indulge my broad and specific expressions of it.

A little encouragement from friends can go a long way: Karen first told me that I should keep writing; Jennifer championed my articles on race and abuse; Scott challenged me to steward big ideas. Gestures like these from many friends kept me writing when I doubted whether anyone cared what I had to say.

For eleven years, part of my ministry to Whitton Avenue Bible Church was an article in the weekly newsletter that I probably spent more time writing than I should have. Yet the feedback I received from friends, mentors, and church members on the email list inspired me to articulate biblical convictions and cultural observations as creatively and helpfully as possible. My years of serving that sweet church family with the other elders shaped me and my writing more than I could have anticipated.

I have dedicated this book to my wife, Rachael, who has

heard me obsess over this topic since the day in 2014 when I walked into our family room from my home office, tore off a piece of art paper from our children's easel, and started writing out every reference to the coming of Jesus in the New Testament letters. When I lost steam for the project over the years or heard crickets from publishers, she lovingly and pointedly told me, "This book needs to be written. God has called you to write it. So write the book." Her belief in me and this book is, humanly speaking, why you now hold it in your hand.

Many professors helped me think through the theological and practical issues this book addresses: Dr. John DelHousaye, who gave me the idea for "The Lord's Appearings" chapter and alerted me to the "violent removal" concept explored in chapters 5 and 9; Dr. Alex Kirk, who gave an exegetically warranted redirection to chapter 6 based on his doctoral work; Dr. Steven Tracy, whose encouragement and wisdom propelled me from the time when this book was a fresh idea. At different stages of writing, Dr. Tom Schreiner and Dr. Richard Gaffin kindly responded to requests for a meal and pointed me in a helpful direction with my theology and exegesis.

Publishing is its own journey. A number of people—from fellow church members who watched me grow up to ministry colleagues to friends—kindly read and gave notes on early drafts. My friend Katelyn Beaty gave me hope and direction from her publishing prowess, and my agent, Keely Boeving, skillfully navigated me through the process. The Zondervan Reflective team has been extraordinary, especially my editor Kyle Rohane, whose love for the church inspired wise suggestions to make this book as beneficial as possible.

Throughout the exhilarating ride from idea to published book, my siblings—Danny, Abby, and Jamie (basically a brother)—have kept me grounded, encouraged, and focused. As you can see in chapter 10, my dad was not here for the ride, because a heart attack in 2018 took him into the presence of Jesus, which is far better (Phil. 1:23). Dad took both the right use of language and the return of Jesus seriously. His imprint on me permeates this book, for which I have the deepest gratitude.

Finally, thank you to Groveton Baptist Church, which I have served since 2016. It is a privilege to learn together in real time what it means to "stir up one another to love and good works . . . and all the more as you see the Day drawing near" (Heb. 10:24–25).

This is a book about Jesus, whom I know by faith, not sight. Jesus, thank you for who you are, what you have done for me, and what you will be and do when you return. The countless hours writing this have left me in awe of you, with bright hope for the day when I see you face to face.

NOTES

1. Brian E. Daley, *The Hope of the Early Church: A Handbook of Patristic Eschatology* (Grand Rapids: Baker Academic, 1991), 39. Daley's excellent survey of Christian hope through the fifth century reveals that Augustine was the most notable of the church fathers who promoted "Christian watchfulness" while acknowledging that we cannot know when Jesus will return (135).

2. John T. Carroll, *The Return of Jesus in Early Christianity* (Peabody: Hendrickson, 2000), 188–90. Joachim's scheme of history was based on the Trinity (the age of the Father, the age of the Son, and the age of the Spirit), while Hippolytus used the scheme of the week, found in both Roman and Jewish thought, where each of the seven days represented a millennium of history.

3. Mark A. Noll, *A History of Christianity in the United States and Canada* (Grand Rapids: Eerdmans, 1992), 193.

4. Charles Spurgeon, "Watching for Christ's Coming," sermon delivered at the Metropolitan Tabernacle, Newington, April 7, 1889, www.spurgeongems.org/sermon/chs2302.pdf. Accessed March 6, 2022.

5. "Jesus Christ's Return to Earth," Pew Research Center, July 14, 2010, www.pewresearch.org/fact-tank/2010/07/14 /jesus-christs-return-to-earth/. Accessed March 6, 2022. The

report also notes, "Fully 58% of white evangelical Christians say Christ will return to earth in this period, by far the highest percentage in any religious group."

6. Horatio G. Spafford, "It Is Well with My Soul."

7. Thomas Obadiah Chisholm, "Great Is Thy Faithfulness."

8. Kevin Mungons, "'Great Is Thy Faithfulness': Discovering the Story behind a Moody Favorite," Moody Bible Institute, August 29, 2019, www.moody.edu/alumni/connect/news /2019/faithfulness-song/. Accessed March 24, 2022.

9. Howard W. Odum, "Religious Folk-Songs of the Southern Negroes" (PhD diss., Clark University, n.d.), Project Gutenberg, March 8, 2012, www.gutenberg.org/files/39078 /39078-h/39078-h.htm (reprinted from *American Journal of Religious Psychology and Education* 3 [July 1909], 265–365). Accessed March 27, 2022.

10. George R. Beasley-Murray, *John*, Word Biblical Commentary (Grand Rapids: Zondervan, 1987), 189.

11. David G. Peterson, *The Acts of the Apostles*, Pillar New Testament Commentary (Grand Rapids: Eerdmans, 2009), 616–17.

12. Daniel Macht, "Bank Robber Demands Cash, Medical Attention: Cops," NBC Connecticut, April 23, 2012, https://www .nbcconnecticut.com/news/national-international/bank-robber -demands-cash-medical-attention-cops/1927399/, and "The Reel Life: Be Willing to Adapt Edition," Casino City Times, May 3, 2012, www.casinocitytimes.com/news/article/the -reel-life-be-willing-to-adapt-edition-200822. Both stories accessed January 16, 2022.

13. Vendelete, "America's Dumbest Criminals," https://steemit .com/steem/@vendelete/america-s-dumbest-criminals. Accessed January 16, 2022.

14. Tankiso Makhetha, "Auto-Lock Ruins Would Be Thief's Plan," IOL, September 10, 2014, www.iol.co.za/news/south-africa /gauteng/auto-lock-ruins-would-be-thiefs-plan-1748510. Accessed January 16, 2022.

15. Bruce K. Waltke with Charles Yu, *An Old Testament Theology: An Exegetical, Canonical, and Thematic Approach* (Grand Rapids: Zondervan, 2007), 292.

16. All three Synoptic Gospels contain this account: Matthew 17:1–9; Mark 9:2–10; Luke 9:28–36.

17. R. T. France, *The Gospel of Matthew*, New International Biblical Commentary on the New Testament (Grand Rapids: Eerdmans, 2007), 647.

18. John Nolland, *Luke 9:21–18:34*, Word Biblical Commentary (Grand Rapids: Zondervan, 1993), 501.

19. Darrell L. Bock, *Acts*, Baker Exegetical Commentary on the New Testament (Grand Rapids: Baker, 2007), 357.

20. Brad Hambrick, gen. ed., *Becoming a Church That Cares Well for the Abused* (Nashville: Broadman and Holman, 2019), 11–12.

21. Richard Bauckham and Trevor Hart, *Hope against Hope: Christian Eschatology at the Turn of the Millennium* (Grand Rapids: Eerdmans, 1999), xii.

22. Chris Davis, "The Privilege of Persecution in Northern India," Gospel Coalition, January 6, 2015, www.thegospelcoalition. org/article/the-privilege-of-persecution-in-northern-india/.

23. To be clear, there is justice to pursue in this life. There is legal action to take, misuse of power to address, political activism to engage in for religious liberty, and advocacy work to be done for abuse prevention and healing. But final justice will not be satisfied until the King returns to set everything right. So while we take appropriate civil and legal action in this life,

we hope fully in the return of our Warrior King, who will afflict those who have afflicted us.

24. Davis, "Privilege of Persecution in Northern India."

25. The account in 1 Samuel 24 of David and his abuser, Saul, displays a posture of forgiveness shared from a safe distance.

26. "'Is taken away,' must refer to an unnatural removal, since in marriage customs of the day it was the guests who departed, not the newly married couple." John Nolland, *Luke 1–9:20*, Word Biblical Commentary (Grand Rapids: Zondervan, 1989), 248. "The idea of the bridegroom being removed from the wedding scene comes as a jarring surprise." Robert A. Guelich, *Mark 1–8:26*, Word Biblical Commentary (Grand Rapids: Zondervan, 1989), 112.

27. φανερόω in Walter Bauer, *A Greek-English Lexicon of the New Testament and Other Early Christian Literature*, ed. Frederick W. Danker, 3rd ed. (Chicago: Univ. of Chicago Press, 2000), 1048.

28. I am indebted to Alex Kirk for the emphasis on Jesus' return as Judge being something Paul welcomed because of the vindication it would bring amid harsh criticism. Alex gave me many helpful notes on this chapter through personal correspondence. His work on these texts in Corinthians can be found in chapters 9 and 10 of his published dissertation, Alexander N. Kirk, *The Departure of an Apostle: Paul's Death Anticipated and Remembered* (Tübingen: Mohr Siebeck, 2015).

29. Ralph P. Martin, *2 Corinthians*, Word Biblical Commentary (Grand Rapids: Zondervan, 1986), 114.

30. See the discussion on these materials in Gordon Fee, *The First Epistle to the Corinthians*, New International Commentary on the New Testament (Grand Rapids: Eerdmans, 1987), 140, and in Anthony Thiselton, *The First Epistle to the Corinthians*,

New International Greek Testament Commentary (Grand Rapids: Eerdmans, 2000), 311–12.

31. David E. Garland, *1 Corinthians*, Baker Exegetical Commentary on the New Testament (Grand Rapids: Baker Academic, 2003), 737.

32. Putting the time-oriented words of these verses side by side, one could conclude that we live in "today" until we reach "the Day."

33. Richard B. Hays, *First Corinthians*, Interpretation: A Bible Commentary for Teaching and Preaching (Louisville: John Knox, 1997), 83.

34. For a more practical and in-depth treatment of church discipline, see Jonathan Leeman, *Church Discipline: How the Church Protects the Name of Jesus* (Wheaton, IL: Crossway, 2012).

35. John Jones, "A Testimony of Restoration," 9Marks, January 9, 2018, www.9marks.org/article/a-testimony-of-restoration. Accessed January 19, 2022.

36. Two particularly helpful resources on fasting are Arthur Wallis, *God's Chosen Fast: A Spiritual and Practical Guide to Fasting* (Fort Washington, PA: CLC Publications, 1975), and John Piper, *A Hunger for God: Desiring God through Fasting and Prayer* (Wheaton, IL: Crossway, 1997).

37. Among the many wonderful resources on Sabbath available, I have been most helped by the treatment in Peter Scazzero, *The Emotionally Healthy Leader: How Transforming Your Inner Life Will Deeply Transform Your Church, Team, and the World* (Grand Rapids: Zondervan, 2015), 143–72.

38. Isaac Watts, "Joy to the World."

39. Garth Lean, *God's Politician: William Wilberforce's Struggle* (Colorado Springs: Helmers and Howard, 1987), 104.

40. Catharina von Schlegel, "Be Still, My Soul," trans. Jane Borthwick.

41. Robert H. Mounce, *The Book of Revelation*, New International Commentary on the New Testament, rev. ed. (Grand Rapids: Eerdmans, 1997), 72.

42. This connection between the parousia in 1 Thessalonians 4 and the theophany on Mount Sinai is treated thoroughly in Joseph Plevnik, *Paul and the Parousia: An Exegetical and Theological Investigation* (Eugene, OR: Wipf and Stock, 2014). This academic work is one of the few books I could find that deals purely with the return of Christ and its intended impact on the Christian life. As the title suggests, Plevnik covers only Paul's writings.

Dig Deeper into
Bright Hope for Tomorrow

Jesus' return is not a puzzle to be solved or a theological position to be affirmed but otherwise ignored. In the *Bright Hope for Tomorrow Video Study*, pastor Chris Davis shows that it is a promised revelation that should captivate your imagination, shape your weekly rhythm, and purify your heart.